THE UNAUTHORIZED GUIDE TO IPHONE®, IPAD®, AND IPOD® REPAIR

A DIY Guide to Extending the Life of Your iDevices!

Timothy L. Warner

D1296767

que®

800 East 96th Street,
Indianapolis, Indiana 46240 USA

The Unauthorized Guide to iPhone®, iPad®, and iPod® Repair

Copyright © 2013 by Pearson Education, Inc.

ISBN-10: 0-7897-5073-2
ISBN-13: 978-0-7897-5073-0

Library of Congress Cataloging-in-Publication Data is on file

Printed in the United States of America
First Printing: May 2013

Trademarks

Warning and Disclaimer

Bulk Sales

Que Publishing offers excellent discounts on this book when ordered in quantity for bulk purchases or special sales. For more information, please contact

U.S. Corporate and Government Sales
1-800-382-3419
corpsales@pearsontechgroup.com

For sales outside of the U.S., please contact

International Sales
international@pearsoned.com

Editor-in-Chief
Greg Wiegand

Executive Editor
Rick Kughen

Development Editor
Rick Kughen

Technical Editor
Walter Galan,
ifixit.com

Managing Editor
Kristy Hart

Senior Project Editor
Lori Lyons

Copy Editor
Charlotte Kughen,
The Wordsmithery
LLC

Indexer
Tim Wright

Proofreader
Kathy Ruiz

Publishing Coordinators
Cindy Teeters
Kristen Watterson

Book Designer
Anne Jones

Compositor
Nonie Ratcliff

Manufacturing Buyer
Dan Uhrig

Contents at a Glance

Table of Contents

About the Author

Timothy L. Warner is an IT professional and technical trainer based in Nashville, TN. As Director of Technology for a progressive high school, he created and managed a self-servicing warranty repair shop for all Apple hardware used at the institution. Warner has been an Apple enthusiast and power user since the original Macintosh was released in 1984. He has worked in nearly every facet of IT, from systems administration and software architecture to technical writing and training. Warner can be reached at tim.warner@cbtnuggets.com.

Dedication

To the most important women in my life: Susan Warner, Zoey Warner, Sherry Warner, and Trish Warner.

Acknowledgments

Publishing a book requires collaboration between many different people. Thanks to my wonderful editor, Rick Kughen, for conceiving the idea for this work. Thanks to the entire Pearson team, especially Lori Lyons, who worked valiantly to get this book out before Apple released another set of products (not an easy feat, I assure you).

Special thanks to Walter Galan and Kyle Wiens from iFixit for their enthusiastic partnership in this endeavor. Thanks to Charlotte Kughen of Wordsmithery LLC for her great suggestions and for making my words flow so nicely.

Thanks to Tom Chick of Intelligent Designs (idez.com) for the technical guidance on the iDevice take-aparts—you have been a great mentor to me over the years.

Thanks to all my family and friends for your continued love and support. Special shout-out to my parents, Larry and Sherry Warner, in whose basement I produced most of this manuscript during an extended family vacation.

We Want to Hear from You!

As the reader of this book, *you* are our most important critic and commentator. We value your opinion and want to know what we're doing right, what we could do better, what areas you'd like to see us publish in, and any other words of wisdom you're willing to pass our way.

We welcome your comments. You can email or write to let us know what you did or didn't like about this book—as well as what we can do to make our books better.

Please note that we cannot help you with technical problems related to the topic of this book.

When you write, please be sure to include this book's title and author as well as your name and email address. We will carefully review your comments and share them with the author and editors who worked on the book.

Email: feedback@quepublishing.com

Mail: Que Publishing
              ATTN: Reader Feedback
              800 East 96th Street
              Indianapolis, IN 46240 USA

Reader Services

Visit our website and register this book at quepublishing.com/register for convenient access to any updates, downloads, or errata that might be available for this book.

Introduction

Have you ever broken an electronic device? In particular, has your iPod, iPhone, or iPad ever taken a tumble, resulting in a cracked screen? Is your iDevice's battery life not what it once was?

How do you ordinarily handle these situations when they occur? Please take comfort in the fact that *you are not obligated to pay Apple's sometimes exorbitant fees for out-of-warranty iDevice replacements.* Instead, you can learn to perform your own repairs!

If you study this book and invest in the proper time, tools, and materials to attain enough practical experience then you can save yourself a lot of money (and even make quite a bit of extra money to boot) performing iDevice repairs for your family, friends, and even the general public.

Do you want to know more? Read on, friend!

What's in This Book

To present all the various ways you can take full control of your iDevices, this book contains 19 chapters. Each chapter walks you through a different aspect of Do-It-Yourself (DIY) iDevice repair, from character traits of the ideal iDevice tech to where to get the best deals on iDevice hardware:

- **Chapter 1, "Why Do It Yourself?"** presents all the reasons why you might want to consider taking screwdriver in hand and performing DIY work on your iDevices.

- **Chapter 2, "The Tools of the Trade,"** is all about understanding what is required of you, from character traits to specific hardware tools, to become an effective iDevice technician.

- **Chapter 3, "Protecting Your iDevice User Data and Settings,"** is where you learn how to ensure that you don't lose any of your precious documents or settings when you perform work on iDevice hardware.

- **Chapter 4, "iDevice Repair Best Practices,"** connects you to the larger computer technician community and makes you fully aware of the tips and tricks professionals use to guarantee a safe work environment.

- **Chapter 5, "iPhone 3GS Disassembly and Reassembly,"** is a great place to begin your iDevice disassembly practice because 3GS hardware is inexpensive and the phones are relatively easy to take apart.

- **Chapter 6, "iPhone 4S Disassembly and Reassembly,"** shows you how easy and (dare I say it) enjoyable it is to work on iPhones; they represent the best Apple iDevices to repair, bar none.

- **Chapter 7, "iPhone 5 Disassembly and Reassembly,"** continues the iPhone DIY love; you'll be pleased to note that with respect to the iPhone, Apple actually made this model of the device easier for us repair techs to disassemble and perform parts replacements.

- **Chapter 8, "iPad 2nd Generation Disassembly and Reassembly,"** presents a full walkthrough on the iPad 2. You'll be unpleasantly surprised to learn how difficult it is to gain entry to these beasts.

- **Chapter 9, "iPad 3rd and 4th Generation Disassembly and Reassembly,"** doesn't have a lot more good news in the screen removal department (iPads are notorious for DIYers in this regard). However, after you have the display off, performing repairs and parts replacements on iPads is largely a breeze.

- **Chapter 10, "iPad mini Disassembly and Reassembly,"** presents how to disassemble and reassemble Apple's smallest iPad model. The good news is that the iPad interior is intelligently designed. The bad news is that the display is difficult to remove and parts are permanently soldered to the logic board.

- **Chapter 11, "iPod touch 4th Generation Disassembly and Reassembly,"** provides proof that Apple doesn't want anybody (including its Apple Store employees) opening any iPod touch device.

- **Chapter 12, "iPod nano 5th and 7th Generation Disassembly and Reassembly,"** takes on the nearly insurmountable task of disassembling an iPod nano without doing more damage in the process. Again, Apple considers all iPods to be disposable devices; I do my best to teach you how to prove Apple wrong.

- **Chapter 13, "Sourcing iDevice Replacement Parts,"** submits strategies for separating the wheat from the chaff, as it were, in terms of finding iDevice replacement parts that actually work. You would be surprised (or not) at the quality variance that exists in the marketplace.

- **Chapter 14, "Addressing Water Damage,"** gives practical tips and tricks for resurrecting an iDevice that has taken a bath against your will. The information in this chapter can save you quite a bit of money at the Apple Store!

- **Chapter 15, "Replacing the Front Display and/or Rear Case,"** shows you how to perform what is by far the most common iDevice repair—replacing the display assembly and/or the rear case.

- **Chapter 16, "Replacing the Battery,"** demonstrates that batteries do indeed have a limited lifetime and it is relatively straightforward, depending upon the model, to replace the battery in your iDevice.

- **Chapter 17, "Replacing the Logic Board and/or Dock Connector,"** teaches you about the logic board, which constitutes the "brains" of any iDevice, and gives you techniques for performing this most fundamental of parts swap-outs.

- **Chapter 18, "Recovering Data from Your Broken iDevice,"** presents clear instructions for retrieving otherwise lost data from crashed, crushed, or otherwise hopelessly damaged iDevices.

- **Chapter 19, "Before You Sell, Donate, or Recycle Your iDevice,"** outlines lots of ways to protect your privacy when you decide to pass your iDevice along to another person.

That's a lot of stuff! Then again, there's a lot you can do with your iDevices. It is my goal as your instructor to make you fully aware of what's possible with your new, secondhand, or seemingly "broken" iPods, iPhones, and iPads.

Who Can Use This Book

You don't have to be a technical expert to use this book; many of the procedures discussed here require nothing more than basic computer skills. It helps if you know your way around electronics or computer hardware, and you'll find out soon enough that this book contains some procedures that require those skills to greater or lesser degrees. But in general, just about anybody can perform most of the hardware and software exercises presented.

As you must know, iDevices are made by Apple. However, you can use iTunes and many other iDevice management tools either on OS X (Mac) or Windows. This book is written for both platforms. In most cases, the procedure is the same; I point out where operating system-specific differences exist.

How to Use This Book

I think you will find this book easy to use and helpful. To that end, I have included some items that help organize and call attention to specific pieces of information.

As you've probably already noticed, this book contains Notes, Tips, and Cautions—all of which are explained here:

NOTE

Notes point out ancillary bits of information that are helpful, but not crucial.

TIP

Tips point out a useful bit of information to help you solve a problem.

CAUTION

Cautions alert you to potential disasters and pitfalls. Don't ignore these!

I've offered many solutions to your iDevice repair problems, but some of these solutions involve software, websites, and services owned by third parties outside my direct control. I've included web addresses (URLs) for those sites when appropriate. To keep long and cryptic URLs under control, I used the is.gd URL shortening service for your convenience. I've tried to ensure that the web addresses in this book are accurate, but given how quickly the Web changes, you might find an address or two that no longer works. I am sorry about that, but with a little Google searching, you can probably find the resource at its new location.

Warning and Disclaimer

While Que, iFixit, and I have made every effort to ensure that the directions provided in this book are complete and accurate, any attempt on the reader's part to perform an iDevice do-it-yourself upgrade or repair is solely at the reader's risk. Even when our instructions are carefully followed, the slightest misstep in disassembly or reassembly could result in further damage or destruction of the iDevice. Also, any attempt to repair or upgrade your iDevice immediately voids any warranty you have through Apple. You've been warned!

There's More Online...

When you need a break from reading, feel free to go online and check out my personal website at www.timwarnertech.com. Here you'll find more information about this book as well as other work I do. And if you have any questions or comments, feel free to email me directly at tim@timwarnertech.com. I do my utmost to answer every email message I receive from my readers and students.

Do It *Your Way*

With all these preliminaries out of the way, it's now time to get started. Put on your reading glasses, fire up your iDevice, and get ready to take complete control of your Apple hardware!

Why Do It Yourself?

If you read the introduction to this book (highly recommended, as it is scintillating reading), you know who my target audience is, and you know exactly what constitutes an iDevice. Given that background, I have a question for you: Why do you want to learn how to repair iDevices? What knowledge or skills do you hope to derive by studying this book?

To be sure, there is money to be made for people with the interest and technical aptitude to repair iDevices, either in or out of warranty. Perhaps you want to be able to brag to your friends in the neighborhood bar, "I'll bet y'all I'm the only person who knows exactly what is inside those iPhones you are all holding!"

In any event, this chapter starts with a presentation of what I consider to be the chief benefits of Do-It-Yourself (DIY) iDevice repair. I would be remiss if I didn't provide coverage of potential disadvantages as well.

You also need to be fully armed at the outset with regard to the hows and whys of Apple hardware warranties. This chapter discusses in great detail how the Apple Hardware Warranty and the AppleCare programs work, as well as how these legal documents fit into your decision to potentially void warranty.

The chapter concludes with some useful tips and tricks for sourcing older and allegedly "broken" iDevice hardware. After all, you probably want to avoid using your current personal or company iPhone as your first candidate for disassembly. I give you excellent ideas for finding perfectly serviceable iDevices that you can resurrect to full working capacity if you want. After you've brought an iDevice back from the dead, what next? Sell them on eBay for a profit? Gift them to your friends and relatives? That's your decision. In the meantime, c'mon—we have work to do.

The Benefits of DIY iDevice Repair

The decision to take apart an iDevice is not one to be taken lightly. As you'll soon read, you have the AppleCare warranty to think about. If your device is still under warranty then removing a single screw means you just violated that warranty. Yes, it is theoretically possible for you to obtain warranty service from Apple if you scrupulously cover your disassembly tracks, but I advise against it (I explain why as we move onward).

The following list summarizes the primary advantages to learning DIY iDevice repair, and the following sections explain each bullet point in detail. Disadvantages are covered in this discussion as well. The primary advantages to learning iDevice repair include

- Saving money
- Fighting back against the "tyranny" of Apple Inc.
- Preparing for a full-time or part-time job as an Apple tech
- Earning extra money (reselling fixed devices, performing repairs)

Saving Money

My twin sister Trish called me up the other day, very upset. "Timmy, my iPad 2 won't charge anymore!" Sure enough, I concluded after performing some diagnostic testing that her Dock connector was bad. Unfortunately, Trish had not purchased AppleCare protection for the device, and she has owned it for more than one year. Thus, the only option she felt she had available was to purchase a new iPad from her local Apple Store.

"Wait a minute, Trish," I told her. "Let me repair that device for you."

"You can do that?" Trish replied, astonished.

"Yep. Give me a few days to get the part in and your iPad should be as good as new."

Within 10 minutes I had placed an order for an OEM (Original Equipment Manufacturer) iPad 2 Dock connector cable, which set me back all of $10. Within 4 days I had the part, and within 20 minutes I had Trish's iPad 2 charging as good as new.

The previous real-life example is a good justification for taking the time and exerting the effort to learn how to repair iDevices. You can definitely save yourself and those around you a substantial amount of money!

The potential downside to this advantage is that you might make a mistake while performing a repair and cause further damage to the device. In this case, you won't save money at all; in fact, a mistake is likely to cost you extra.

The ways to ward against this problem are to practice on iDevices that you don't plan to actually use. You'll find you are much more willing to experiment and learn iDevice repair best practices the hard way when you aren't invested in the utility of that device. Later in this chapter I share some places where you can check to find deeply discounted iDevices that you can add to your training environment.

Fighting Back Against the "Tyranny" of Apple

In my experience, some folks get awfully bent out of shape over Apple Inc.'s business model. Some iOS developers bristle at having to submit their apps to Apple for approval, much less having the Apple Store be their only sales outlet.

Apple makes it nearly impossible for non-Apple employees to perform warranty repairs on iDevices. Thus, we tinkerers and enthusiasts need to work around Apple's "walled garden" if we want to succeed in our endeavor.

Going further, some iDevice owners jailbreak their devices in order to free the hardware and software from Apple's usage limitations. Read Chapter 3, "Protecting Your iDevice User Data and Settings," to discover more about jailbreaking.

Apple designs, sells, and supports its own hardware and software. Thus, it is within Apple's right to lay down the law with regard to what people who are not Apple staff can and cannot do to our iDevices. That said, we are free to tweak, jailbreak, or hack away on our own iDevices so long as we are aware of the possible consequences of doing so.

Those "consequences" represent the disadvantage of this philosophical advantage. If Apple discovers that you opened an iDevice then the company will formally void your warranty and you have to pay out-of-pocket for a replacement device. This same result occurs if you attempt to submit a jailbroken iDevice for warranty service without resetting the iOS firmware first.

Preparing to Become an Apple Tech

As I stated in the previous section, Apple exerts the strictest control over the sale and support of its iDevices. The bottom line is that if you want to perform warranty repair on iDevices (which gives you access to Apple's GSX online service portal and the ability to order parts directly from Apple), you need to be employed at one of the following types of business:

- An Apple Store
- iOS Direct Service Program shop
- Apple Authorized Service Provider
- Apple Consultants Network Partner

The Apple Store

As you probably know, the Apple Store is Apple's retail presence. These are brick-and-mortar stores spread all over the world. Alternatively, Apple maintains an online Apple Store at http://store.apple.com, from which you can submit warranty repair requests and purchase new stuff.

Apple's tech support personnel in the retail channel are known as Apple Geniuses. These privileged folks have access to all the glorious Apple internal diagnostic tools. They are the agents who assess your iDevice before determining whether warranty coverage is in effect and whether you'll be issued a replacement.

> **NOTE**
>
> **Replacing Is Easier Than Fixing**
>
> If you've ever taken your iDevice to the Apple Genius Bar for warranty service, you doubtless discovered that staff members almost always issue a replacement device instead of assigning a tech to perform a part replacement. In fact, I have never once heard of an occasion where an on-premises tech performed a parts replacement in an Apple Store.

iOS Direct Service Program

The iOS Direct Service Program is available to enterprise organizations, schools, and government agencies who own at least 100 Apple iOS devices and who seek to perform their own hardware maintenance.

As an information technology (IT) professional, I can attest that iDevices are not made specifically for business use. However, many institutions do issue and maintain iDevices and therefore need to maintain those devices.

Essentially, access to the iOS Direct Service Program allows a business access to Apple diagnostic tools and gives them the ability to order replacement units. Are you seeing a pattern here, friends? Apple really does not want anybody—even their own Apple Store techs—monkeying around with the internals of their iDevices. It is simply more cost-effective to issue a replacement and perhaps resell the failed unit after it's been refurbished.

Apple Authorized Service Provider (AASP)

The golden credential for an individual or business who seeks to perform warranty repair on iDevices is the Apple Authorized Service Provider (AASP). However, now that Apple Stores have such deep penetration in the world, Apple has suspended applications to this program, at least as of this writing in late 2012. Surprised? You shouldn't be.

In Nashville, TN, where I live, we have a long-standing "mom and pop" AASP called Mac Authority (http://www.macauthority.com). Nashville is Music City, U.S.A., and many (perhaps most) music industry folks use Apple products. Thus, Mac Authority had a thriving business. At least until the Apple Store moved into town.

The good news is that at least Apple isn't revoking AASP status to businesses that currently hold the credential.

Apple Consultants Network (ACN)

The Apple Consultants Network (ACN) (http://consultants.apple.com) is a membership-only directory of individuals and businesses that are authorized by Apple to perform warranty work on Apple desktop and mobile hardware and software.

ACN partners generate a lot of business through referrals from—you guessed it—Apple Stores. I have a good friend who works for an ACN member shop. Most of their enterprise work comes through the city's local Apple Store. A business contacts the Apple Store looking for advice on deploying Macs in a business network, and the Apple Store refers the company to my friend's shop, who specializes in that type of work.

I have more to say about the ACN in Chapter 2, "The Tools of the Trade," which discusses Apple certifications in greater detail.

I gave you all of this background information so that you'd know that by learning how to repair iDevices you have plenty of options open to you as a technician.

If there is a corresponding disadvantage to this advantage, it is the fact that you must play by Apple's rules if you want to perform warranty repair work. Some people complain that this option makes them feel like an "Apple drone," and they therefore go the rogue route and perform strictly out-of-warranty repair work for their clients.

Earning Extra Money

Two of the cool things about information technology are the following:

- It is privileged knowledge that is beyond the reach of most people
- People are willing to pay you good money for you to share some of your privileged knowledge

Your startup costs for becoming a part-time or full-time iDevice technician are the following:

- Technician tools
- Stock of replacement parts
- Time and effort in building your skills

The technician tools, to which all of Chapter 2 is devoted, represent a one-time cost that should be recouped after your first few repairs. The stock of replacement parts represents an investment against future work. So long as you select your parts carefully (and I teach you all about that later), you should find use for them in relatively short order.

The third up-front cost is simply the time and effort required for you to build your skills. The next chapter breaks down exactly what those skills are and how you can most efficiently develop them.

The potential downside to this advantage is similar to the first advantage; namely, if you make a mistake, correcting that mistake might wind up costing you money. For instance, a good friend of mine who works as a self-employed iDevice tech accidentally broke the front glass panel of a customer's iPad while reassembling the unit after a repair. Guess who incurred the cost of the replacement glass?

iDevices—A Roster

Now is as good a time as any to take a closer look at iDevices from a comparative standpoint. Apple's iDevice portfolio has become substantial; to that end, the following sections describe the barebones characteristics of each generation and identify comparative trends. After this initial discussion, I limit our iDevice scope for the rest of this book (and explain why I've done so).

iPod

The iPod is a portable media player that has no built-in Internet access. The iPod Classic is the prototypical iPod. These bad boys include a mechanical hard drive (!), which means that one good drop makes your music collection (at least on the device) go bye-bye.

Apple released six generations of the iPod Classic, the sixth generation (see Figure 1.1) being introduced on September 5, 2007, with 80-, 120-, and 160-GB models.

FIGURE 1.1 iPod Classic, 6th generation. (Photo courtesy of Apple, Inc.)

The iPod Shuffle is the most affordable of the iDevice line. The Shuffle is meant as a low-budget, low-functionality media player. These devices have no screen to speak of, which means you must manage the device content exclusively from within iTunes.

Apple manufactured four generations of the iPod Shuffle, the last of which was released on September 1, 2010 and has a 2-GB capacity (see Figure 1.2).

NOTE

No Moving Parts

All iDevices with the exception of the iPod Classic employ solid state flash memory for persistent storage, meaning there are no moving parts. Solid-state drives work under the same principle as memory cards and thumb drives. Mechanical hard drives in these devices, with all of their moving parts, would be a very bad idea indeed!

FIGURE 1.2   iPod Shuffle, 4th generation. (Photo courtesy of Apple, Inc.)

The **iPod nano** began life as a little media player Apple called the iPod mini. The mini consisted of two generations, the second of which was released on February 22, 2005 and had 4 GB or 6 GB capacities.

NOTE

For the Editors Among You

I want to point out that while it might look funny to use lowercase letters when typing "iPod mini," "iPod nano," and "iPod touch," rest assured that we are using the product names just as Apple uses them. Given that we're voiding warranties and going where Apple doesn't want us to go, the least we can do is refer to their product names properly.

The mini and nano models were essentially scaled-down versions of the iPod Classic. The main user interface for the Classic, Shuffle, mini, and nano is the scroll wheel. Personally, I love the scroll wheel as a navigational device. In point of fact, my favorite of all iPod models, including the touch, is the iPod nano 5th generation.

It is also worth noting that the Shuffle and the nano were the first iPods to use solid-state disk storage instead of super-old-school magnetic hard drives like the Classic. The main benefit of solid-state disks is that there are no moving parts, so the hard drives are much less likely to suffer damage during a device drop.

Speaking of generations, Apple manufactured seven generations of the nano, the latest of which was released on October 12, 2012 (see Figure 1.3). Unfortunately for me, the sixth and seventh generation nanos lost the tactile scroll wheel and instead use a capacitive touch screen like the iPod touch, iPhone, and iPad.

NOTE

Fancy Schmancy

"Capacitive touch screen" is just an overly complicated term used to describe a touch-sensitive display panel like we use on all modern iDevices.

FIGURE 1.3   iPod nano, 7th generation. (Photo courtesy of Apple, Inc.)

iPod touch

The iPod touch is essentially an iPhone without the cell phone capability. In point of fact, former Apple CEO Steve Jobs called the iPod touch "training wheels" for the iPhone. The market for the iPod touch is people who either are not in a position to switch their cellular service to the iPhone, or for non-iPhone users who want to leverage the neat features offered by the iPhone and its mobile operating system, Apple iOS.

Table 1.1 summarizes the major points of comparison among the five generations of the iPod touch. Figure 1.4 shows you what the iPod touch 5th generation looks like.

TABLE 1.1   iPod touch Comparison Matrix

Generation	Release Date	Capacities (GB)	CPU Core	RAM	Screen Resolution
1st	September 5, 2007	8, 16, 32	ARM 400MHz	128MB	320×480
2nd	September 9, 2008	8, 16, 32	ARM 533MHz	128MB	320×480
3rd	September 9, 2009	32, 64	ARM 600MHz	256MB	320×480
4th	September 9, 2010	8, 16, 32, 64	Apple A4 1GHz	256MB	960×640
5th	September 12, 2012	32, 64	Apple A5	512MB	1136×640

All of the iPod touch models are Wi-Fi only. Generations 1 through 4 offer 802.11b/g wireless connectivity, and the 5th gen iPod touch supports 802.11b/g/n connectivity.

I talk about this subject ad nauseam later in this book, but I need to tell you right here at the outset that Apple considers iPod touches to be disposable units. When you perform repairs, you'll learn that iPod touches have most of their internal components permanently soldered to the logic board. Apple's focus on disposability for iPod touches is galling to many, including myself, because these devices are not cheap.

iPhone

The iPhone is the flagship of the iDevice product line. It is a smartphone, which is a fancy term to describe a cell phone that includes various other modes of communication, collaboration, and media playback. The comparison matrix in Table 1.2 shows that Apple has aligned the hardware between the iPhone and the iPod touch very closely from generation to generation. See Figure 1.5 to see the device in all its glory.

Because iPhone generations prior to the 3GS have gone the way of the dodo, I have limited the iPhone comparison to models beginning with the iPhone 3GS. For that matter, the advent of the iPhone 5 in September 2012 rendered the iPhone 3GS largely irrelevant. Regardless, production of the iPhone 3GS was discontinued on June 4, 2010.

FIGURE 1.4   iPod touch, 5th generation. (Photo courtesy of Apple, Inc.)

At the very least, you can purchase 3GS models rather inexpensively and use them for practice as you develop your iDevice repair skills. Moreover, a 3GS is an excellent candidate for use as an iPod touch, as it has the same capabilities.

TABLE 1.2   iPhone Comparison Matrix

Generation	Release Date	Capacities (GB)	CPU Core	RAM	Screen Resolution
iPhone 3GS	July 19, 2009	8, 16, 32	ARM Cortex-A8 833MHz	256MB	320×480
iPhone 4	June 24, 2010	8, 16, 32	Apple A4 1GHz	512MB	960×640
iPhone 4S	October 14, 2011	16, 32, 64	Apple A5 1GHz (dual-core)	512MB	960×640
iPhone 5	September 21, 2012	16, 32, 64	Apple A6 1.2GHz	1GB	1136×640

FIGURE 1.5　iPhone 5. (Photo courtesy of Apple, Inc.)

iPad

The iPad is a tablet (also called slate) computer. When Apple released the iPad, many skeptics called the device an "overgrown iPhone." Boy, how wrong those skeptics were! In point of fact, my iPad 3rd generation is my most frequently used iDevice—I even use it more than the iPhone that I carry in my pocket.

The iPad is so versatile: I keep it by my side as a ready reference source for answering any question that pops into my head. The device is an eReader par excellence, and the Retina display in the 3rd generation model is simply stunning.

Apple manufactures both Wi-Fi-only models as well as those with Wi-Fi/carrier network connectivity. In the U.S., you need to be sure to purchase the correct iPad model (read more on model specifics in Chapter 4, "iDevice Repair Best Practices"):

- iPad 2nd generation Wi-Fi only
- iPad 2nd generation Wi-Fi + 3G (AT&T)
- iPad 2nd generation Wi-Fi + 3G (Verizon)

- iPad 3rd generation Wi-Fi only
- iPad 3rd generation Wi-Fi + 4G (AT&T)
- iPad 3rd generation Wi-Fi + 4G (Verizon)
- iPad 4th generation Wi-Fi only
- iPad 4th generation Wi-Fi + LTE (AT&T)
- iPad 4th generation Wi-Fi + LTE (Verizon)
- iPad 4th generation Wi-Fi + LTE (Sprint)
- iPad mini Wi-Fi only
- iPad mini Wi-Fi + LTE (AT&T)
- iPad mini Wi-Fi + LTE (Verizon)
- iPad mini Wi-Fi + LTE (Sprint)

Of course, a contract is required in order to activate cellular service; for current pricing details see the Verizon, AT&T, and Sprint websites.

Table 1.3 compares the manifold iPad models for you. Please note that Apple has already discontinued the 1st and 3rd generation iPads—these models exist in the table for historical and comparison purposes. Figure 1.6 shows you a picture of the 3rd generation iPad.

TABLE 1.3 iPad Comparison Matrix

Generation	Release Date	Capacities (GB)	CPU Core	RAM	Screen Resolution
iPad	April 3, 2010	16, 32, 64	Apple A4 1GHz	256MB	1024×768
iPad 2	March 11, 2011	16, 32, 64	Apple A5 1GHz (dual-core)	512MB	1024×768
iPad 3rd generation	March 16, 2012	16, 32, 64	Apple A5X 1GHz (dual-core)	1GB	2048×1536
iPad 4th generation	November 2, 2012	16, 32, 64	Apple A6X 1.4GHz (dual core)	1GB	2048×1536
iPad mini	November 2, 2012	16, 32, 64	Apple A5 1GHz (dual core)	512MB	1024×768

FIGURE 1.6   iPad, 3rd generation. (Photo courtesy of Apple, Inc.)

Limiting Our Scope

One of the first things you'll observe as you work through the remainder of this book is that I cover only selected iDevice models in depth. Why?

The bottom line and sad truth, friends, is that iDevices become unofficially obsolete faster than any of us would like. For example, I checked the AT&T and Verizon websites just now, and I discovered that neither cellular carrier sells the iPhone 3GS anymore. Apple has formally discontinued the 1st and 3rd generation iPads as well.

Moreover, with the exception of the touch, none of the iPods are worth the time, effort, and money it takes to perform a parts replacement. One of my good friends who has contacts within the iPod development team at Apple told me that Apple considers all non-touch iPods to be "disposable" hardware.

Finally, note that I don't use the "G" designation unless the product brand name includes it. For instance, you can speak of the iPhone 3G or iPhone 3GS because that's what Apple called those iDevices. By contrast, I call the iPhone 4 as such and not "iPhone 4G" as you sometimes see online. The reasons? (a) Apple doesn't include 4G in that model's name; and (b) the iPhone 4 does not support 4G carrier networks.

Likewise, I refer to the iPod touch 5th generation as either "5th generation" or "5th gen" because I don't want to cause confusion. Recall, of course, that 2G, 3G, and 4G are terms for cellular networks! You need to keep your terminology straight here, people. If you are to serve others as a knowledgeable, credible iDevice tech then you need to use the correct nomenclature.

Apple Warranties and You

It's time to turn our attention to the subject of Apple warranties. Before you remove a single screw from your iDevice, you need to answer the following questions:

- Is my iDevice still under AppleCare or AppleCare+?
- If I'm still under warranty, why do I want to disassemble the unit myself?
- If I'm not still under warranty, am I confident that I can complete the repair?

In general, I suggest that you not attempt any DIY operations on a device that remains under AppleCare or AppleCare+. If you are out of warranty, then it's a crapshoot—your decision should be guided by the amount of money you'd spend DIY versus trading in your broken unit for a replacement.

But I get a little bit ahead of myself. Let's discuss how the warranties work.

Apple Hardware Warranty

When you purchase an iDevice, you are given 90 days of free telephone technical support and one calendar year (from the purchase date) of hardware protection.

CAUTION

Read the Warranty!

Take some time to read the Apple Hardware Warranties (https://www.apple.com/legal/warranty/) so that you are fully aware of what iDevice damage is covered and what is not covered.

The Apple Hardware Warranty covers

...defects in materials and workmanship when used normally in accordance with Apple's published guidelines...Apple's published guidelines include but are not limited to information contained in technical specifications, user manuals and service communications.

Specifically, the Apple Hardware Warranty covers all of your iDevice hardware, including

- The unit itself
- The battery
- Earphones
- Cabling

So, basically, if your iDevice malfunctions in the space of one year and the reason for that malfunction lies in the hardware itself then you can bring the iDevice to an Apple Store to be issued a replacement unit.

CAUTION

User-Inflicted Damage Not Covered

Please note that the Apple Hardware Warranty does not in any way cover user-generated damage to the device. If you drop your iPhone and shatter the back glass then you are on the hook for the full cost of a replacement. If you broke off a piece of your iPad charger cable inside the Dock connector, then you are similarly hosed.

Speaking of replacement costs, out-of-warranty iDevice swap-outs have fixed prices that are set by Apple corporate and are adhered to uniformly by all Apple Stores. As of this writing, the following summarizes the standard iDevice replacement costs:

- **iPhone 4:** $150
- **iPhone 4S:** $199
- **iPad 2:** $250
- **iPad 3rd Gen:** $299

A common question folks have when they open their wallets for an out-of-warranty (or heck, even an in-warranty) iDevice replacement is, "Am I receiving a new or refurbished device?"

The answer is surprising: All iDevice swap-outs in Apple Stores are with new hardware. Apple is remarkably candid when it does offer refurbished hardware either online or in a physical Apple Store. You'll find refurbished devices (typically older-generation hardware) in a separate area of the storefront.

AppleCare+

Apple charges customers an extra $99 for AppleCare+ (called "AppleCare Plus"), and in my experience the warranty is worth every penny. The plan is available for all iDevices, and provides you with the following benefits:

■ Extends the default 90 days of complimentary telephone support to two years from date of iDevice purchase

■ Extends the Apple Hardware Warranty two years from date of purchase

■ Provides two years of enhanced coverage

The third bullet point bears a bit of extra explanation. Apple calls AppleCare for iPod touches the "AppleCare Protection Plan," and its AppleCare for iPhones and iPads "AppleCare+." What's the difference?

The main difference between these warranty plans is that AppleCare+ covers you for up to two incidents of accidental damage, each incident being subject to a $49 service fee.

Given how many iPhones I've broken through drops and the like, this two-incident benefit makes AppleCare+ infinitely worthwhile.

Why Apple doesn't offer AppleCare+ for iPod touches is a mystery to me. Then again, much of Apple is, to me (and to quote Winston Churchill) an "enigma shrouded in a mystery."

Is there a catch to AppleCare+? Sort of. Your best bet is to purchase and activate AppleCare+ at the time you purchase your iDevice. However, Apple gives you 30 days after your purchase date to buy and activate an AppleCare+ plan.

TIP

AppleCare+ Available at Apple Store

You can purchase AppleCare+ at the online Apple Store. In any event, please be sure to read all of the details of AppleCare+ at https://www.apple.com/support/products/ so you can say that you performed due diligence on the matter.

Oh, one other thing before we move on. In case you were wondering where the provisions against DIY repairs exactly are in the Apple Hardware Warranty and AppleCare+ contracts, allow me to point it out.

The following extract is taken from the Apple Hardware Warranty for the iPhone 5 (https://www.apple.com/legal/warranty/), in the "What is Not Covered in This Warranty?" section, paragraph 2:

> *The warranty does not apply to damage caused by service (including upgrades and expansions) performed by anyone who is not a representative of Apple or an Apple Authorized Service Provider ("AASP").*

The following extract is taken from the AppleCare+ terms and conditions (https://www.apple.com/legal/applecare/applecareplusforiphone.html), section 4.2, item ii, part d:

The Plan does not apply to damage caused by service (including upgrades and expansions) if such was performed by anyone who is not a representative of Apple or an Apple Authorized Service Provider ("AASP").

There you have it. Consider yourself duly warned! I cover how you can check the warranty status of a given iDevice in Chapter 4. For now, though, I want to round out this chapter by telling you where you can source used iDevice hardware for your learning pleasure.

Finding Old, "Broken" iDevices

Earlier I suggested that before you start tearing apart your equipment or anyone else's, you'd be wise to invest in one or more iDevices that you can use exclusively for learning purposes. These are iPhones, iPads, and iPod touches that have no daily usage value to you or anyone around you, and you would not be heartbroken if you brick the device.

NOTE

Brick = Dead

Incidentally, *brick* is a slang term that you hear quite a bit in iDevice DIY circles. To "brick" an iDevice is to render it permanently inoperable. The good news is that I have found it nearly (but not totally) impossible to brick an iDevice unless you physically destroy the chassis.

Thus, the question arises: Where can you find some used iDevice hardware to play around with? The good news is that I have plenty of quality sources to share with you.

Pawn or Secondhand Shops

I have found some great deals on iDevices by browsing my local secondhand stores and pawn shops. It is a great relief knowing that you aren't trusting the store dealer to sell you a fully functional iDevice. Whether the device is functional is beside the point at this stage of your development as a tech. You just need to get your hands on the hardware itself. Check out Figure 1.7 to see the practice iDevice hardware I procured for less than $100.

Some iDevices might have some dents or scratches, but you don't need to care about cosmetics. And you can forget about the secondhand shop offering you information on warranty—you have to ferret all of those details yourself.

FIGURE 1.7   I paid a total of $75 for this very serviceable iPhone 3GS and "gently dented" iPod nano 5th generation.

eBay or Craigslist

I offer eBay (http://ebay.com) and Craigslist (http://craigslist.org) to you because they are legitimate sources for used iDevices. That said, I warn you to be careful in how you approach these transactions.

Please pay close attention to buyer comments for any eBay sellers with whom you plan to do business. Also, be sure to meet anybody from Craigslist not at your home, but instead in a well-lighted, public location. Don't take any chances just because you are hot to get your hands on some used iDevice gear!

With respect to eBay, I suggest that you take advantage of the advanced search options (http://www.ebay.com/sch/ebayadvsearch/?rt=nc) to limit the scope of your search. For instance, when I search for items on eBay I set my advanced search criteria to return only items that are listed as "Buy it Now" and include free shipping. You can see some sample eBay search results in Figure 1.8.

You can save yourself considerable time and money by using eBay and Craigslist "power user" tricks. For instance, try running the following search strings at eBay or Craigslist:

- iphone for parts
- ipod broken
- ipad cracked

You can find some excellent deals on "broken" iDevices on eBay if you know how to perform an advanced search.

FIGURE 1.8   eBay search results for scrap iPhones.

Craigslist is cool because you don't necessarily have to limit yourself to your local area. As long as the iDevice seller is willing to accept payment remotely and mail you the device, you can do business with any Craigslist seller.

Before you delve too deeply into Craigslist, please take some time to read the site's guidelines on avoiding scams. You can find the guidelines at http://www.craigslist.org/about/scams.

Amazon.com

I was tempted to lump Amazon.com into the same section as eBay and Craigslist, but Amazon deserves its own section. You can find far, far more than brand-new products at Amazon.com. It is actually a bit frightening to me how comprehensive Amazon's reach is, in between its own stock and their enormous network of public and private resellers.

I revisit good ol' Amazon.com later when I talk about sourcing iDevice repair parts.

Yard Sales or Flea Markets

In my experience, the likelihood of finding used iDevices at a garage sale, estate sale, yard sale, or flea market is pretty low. The overwhelming popularity of Apple hardware is such that you would be hard-pressed to see anybody offering these products in these environments. If they did then the devices would probably be snapped up almost instantly.

Nevertheless, if someone in your life frequents these types of marketplaces then I suggest that you ask him or her to keep an eye out for used iDevice gear. I asked my parents, who are inveterate bargain-hunters, to do this for me. No luck yet, but you never know what the future will bring!

Friends, Family, and Colleagues

Never underestimate the power of social networking. Post a Facebook status update asking your friends if anybody has an iDevice that they don't need anymore. Many people, for unexplained reasons, hold onto their old iDevices when they move to a more recent model. Why not convince the people in your life to turn their supposedly "broken" or "outdated" devices into cash?

Bulletin Boards

In my community in Nashville, TN, there is a thriving physical bulletin board in the vestibule of the local Kroger grocery store. All you have to do to post an announcement is to speak to the store manager and ask for his permission. A *lot* of people stop to check out that bulletin board as they enter or leave the store.

The same rule applies to public bulletin boards at universities, community centers, gyms, shopping malls, churches, and the like. Spend a few minutes whipping up a WANTED announcement, print several copies, and post them (with permission) to as many public bulletin boards as possible. You'll find plenty of people willing to sell you their old iDevices. To that point, there may come a day when you post announcements advertising your iDevice repair services to the general public!

We can also turn to electronic "bulletin boards" in the form of newspaper classified ads or community websites. Be creative, and your hard work will pay off dividends.

The Tools of the Trade

This chapter discusses what is required of you—physically, psychologically, and in terms of materials—for you to be a successful iDevice Do-It-Yourself (DIY) technician. Some specific questions that might be on your mind right now include the following:

- How much of a "techie" do I have to be to learn DIY iDevice repair?
- Do I have to solder anything?
- How much money do the repair tools cost?

We cover all the preceding questions and more. Let's start with discovering what is required of you to succeed at iDevice repair.

What Does It Take to Become an iDevice Technician?

I've been working with Apple hardware since the first Macintosh was introduced on January 24, 1984. However, it wasn't until I earned a bachelor's degree in biology, a master's degree in education, and was unsuccessful in finding a job as a public school science teacher that I had my career epiphany:

"Hey, you have a knack for computers. Why not consider going into the field full time?"

I entered the information technology field in 1997 and never looked back. Given my experience and the benefit of hindsight, I can say with confidence that anybody can succeed as an iDevice repair technician if they work diligently to develop the following three success factors:

- Interest
- Aptitude
- Practice

You are reading this book, which tells me that you are genuinely interested in the subject matter. That's a good thing. The way you'll learn your degree of aptitude (native ability) in iDevice repair will emerge after you take screwdriver in hand and begin to practice (which, of course, is the third essential ingredient to my success formula).

Character Traits

There are five character traits that you must have if you want to have any kind of enjoyable time working on Apple hardware:

- **Patience**—You will learn before too long that Apple makes the absolute most use of the limited space inside of an iPod touch or iPhone. There is literally no wasted space inside those chassis. Moreover, the screws involved are so tiny that dropping one on a pile carpet (not that you should be working in a carpeted room; more on that later) means you pretty much lost the screw forever. Thus, iDevice repair is not for high-strung individuals. You need to be methodical and relaxed. You need to be patient, and take the disassembly and reassembly steps one at a time.

- **Dexterity**—As I just told you, the components inside iDevices, even larger ones such as the iPad, are delicate and extraordinarily small. Although specialty tools can help in this regard, you nonetheless need to have a certain baseline level of hand-eye coordination and fine motor skills in order to successfully operate on iDevices.

TIP

I Can See Clearly Now

Believe me, there is no shame in using a magnifying glass. In point of fact, using a work light with an integrated magnifier (discussed later on in this chapter) is actually highly recommended.

- **Tenacity**—Tenacity means "persistent determination." When the going gets rough during a disassembly or parts replacement procedure, there is no "giving up." If you need to take a break and get a breath of fresh air to refocus then you certainly should. However, the work will be waiting for you when you return. Those iDevices won't put themselves back together. The combination of patience and tenacity is one of the critical success factors to any computer repair technician, much less an individual who specializes in Apple mobile hardware.

- **Organization**—Let me be frank: If you go into an iDevice disassembly without a plan for organizing screws and parts, then you will find yourself in a world of hurt from which you might not be able to recover. Do you notice how these required character traits work together? It takes patience and tenacity to work out an organizational system to guide your iDevice repair processes. The good news is that maintaining an organized work environment isn't rocket science. By the conclusion of this chapter you will understand how to set up your work area to minimize the "one stray part left over" pitfall of iDevice repair.

■ **Confidence/Courage**—Finally, you need to be confident and courageous to undertake iDevice repair. When someone trusts you to examine and repair his iDevice, he's giving you a significant compliment about your ability. Regardless of whether you feel confident or courageous, you must (as William James suggests in *The Varieties of Religious Experience*) *act as if* you are confident and courageous, and the rest will follow.

Technical Ability

Now that you know what kind of character traits you need, it's time to address the question of technical ability. In order to succeed as an iDevice technician, you need to possess the following software skills:

■ Basic familiarity with the Apple iOS

■ Basic computer literacy (Mac or PC)

iOS is the mobile operating system used by iPhones, iPod touches, iPads, and the 2nd generation Apple TV. You don't have to be an iDevice power user to perform hardware repair. However, having those skills certainly benefits you from a diagnostic and troubleshooting perspective.

Please consider purchasing a recommended book or two on iOS tips and tricks. You will doubtless find that they come in handy one way or the other.

TIP

Recommended Read

If you want to hone your iOS skills, there are a lot of books out there that will do the trick, though this one is particularly good: *iPad and iPhone Tips and Tricks* (Covers iOS 6 on iPad, iPad mini, and iPhone), 2nd Edition, by Jason Rich (ISBN-10: 0-7897-5096-1).

By "basic computer literacy" I speak of your ability to successfully navigate a desktop operating system. It does not matter whether your operating system platform is OS X or Microsoft Windows; as you doubtless know, iTunes and iCloud client software runs on both operating systems equally well.

You should be familiar with mouse and keyboard navigation, how to copy and move files, and how to mount and eject external devices.

In my experience, you should do what you can to gain an equal level of familiarity with both OS X and Windows because as a Windows-based iDevice technician you might be called to troubleshoot an iDevice that synchronizes with OS X, and vice versa.

Obtaining iDevice Technician Tools

Something that is almost always a wake-up call for aspiring iDevice technicians is that you can't simply visit your local hardware store and expect to find the tools you need. Apple makes it difficult by design for you to open iDevice cases and remove components.

Why do you think Apple plays this game? Well, it's simple, really. Recall the discussion on Apple warranties in Chapter 1, "Why Do It Yourself?" that the opening of an iDevice case immediately voids the warranty. The bottom line is that Apple does not want non-Apple personnel horsing around with its hardware.

A good example of this position against iDevice tampering is the pentalobe screw. The iPhone 4 was the first iDevice to use these custom-designed tamper-resistant screws to protect the outer case. You can see the shape of the pentalobe screw head in Figure 2.1. The good news is that you can purchase pentalobe screwdrivers inexpensively from a number of third-party sources.

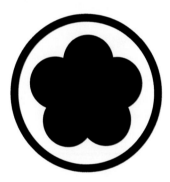

FIGURE 2.1 The pentalobe screw head. (This image was created by Ruudjah2 and is licensed under the Creative Commons Attribution 3.0 Unported license: http://is.gd/93B1MS)

Sources for iDevice Tech Tools

Is there anything that Amazon.com does not sell? Navigate to the Amazon.com Cell Phones & Accessories department and take a look at its Replacement Parts section. There you can find vendor links to any iDevice tools and replacement parts you'll ever need.

You can also perform an advanced search on eBay.com to locate iDevice parts and tools.

Parts quality can vary significantly between suppliers—some eBay, or even Amazon sellers, sell subpar parts. Read customer reviews to ensure you purchase from reputable sellers on eBay or Amazon. Even if a seller has positive past reviews, however, their next batch of parts may be defective, and they will still sell them—either unknowingly or knowingly. By contrast, iFixit tests each and every part before offering them up for sale.

With regard to dedicated third-party sources for iDevice tools and parts, the two companies I have done business with and heartily recommend to you are the following:

- iFixit.com
- iCracked.com

> ## NOTE
>
> **More on Replacement Parts Later**
>
> I delve more into specific suggestions with regard to purchasing iDevice replacement parts in Chapter 13, "Sourcing iDevice Replacement Parts." For now I'm staying focused strictly on sourcing technician tools.

Some third-party sources that I have not yet used but receive good reviews are

- eTechParts.com
- iPartsRepair.com
- cnn.cn
- powerbookmedic.com

Without further ado, it's time to begin building your technician's toolkit!

ESD Safety Equipment

Electrostatic discharge (ESD), also called static electricity, is a very real threat to the safety of all electronic equipment. Did you know that a static charge of as little as 10 volts (V) could damage integrated circuit (IC) components? Hint: You can't even feel a 10V charge, so you don't know you fried your electronics device until you completed the repair or upgrade and try to power it on. You need to be hit with a charge of at least 1,500V even to perceive the electricity.

Some people dismiss the idea of ESD damage and consequently take no precautions against it. Please don't fall into that trap. When I was a computer repair newbie I once built a computer on my carpeted living room floor. As expected, I zapped the motherboard and wasted a couple hundred dollars in the space of two minutes.

Chapter 4, "iDevice Repair Best Practices," covers environmental issues that promote ESD safety. For now you need to know what you need to purchase in order to facilitate an ESD-safe workbench. Here's the deal: ESD builds up on our bodies. You need to prevent that ESD from reaching your delicate iDevice components. Thus, the recommended current flow is as follows:

Your body ==> Antistatic wrist strap ==> Antistatic work mat ==> Ground

Figure 2.2 shows an antistatic work mat and wrist strap.

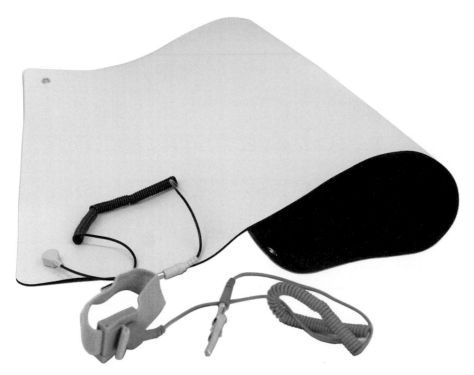

FIGURE 2.2   Antistatic work mat and wrist strap.

Metal in your antistatic wrist strap makes contact with your skin, which conducts the ESD away from your body. Because the antistatic wrist strap is grounded (connected) to the mat, the mat receives discharged ESD both from your body and from the electronic components that lay on that mat. Finally, the mat discharges to whichever ground source you've selected.

There exists much controversy as to what specific type of ground you should use for your ESD work mat. Most techs, myself included, ground to the household AC ground wire by linking the mat's copper ring connector to the ground screw of a household electrical outlet. You can see an excellent schematic drawing of how this ESD connection workflow functions by visiting the Indoff blog post "ESD Workstations" at http://is.gd/04s4aK.

Screwdrivers

As previously discussed, disassembling iDevices requires you to use specialty screwdrivers. Perhaps the two most important screwdrivers for your toolkit are the Phillips #00 and the pentalobe.

You also need small flathead screwdrivers. Rather than sourcing a few select specialty screwdrivers, I instead suggest that you purchase a screwdriver kit that is dedicated to iDevice/small electronics repair. I purchased my own screwdriver kit (see Figure 2.3) from iFixit, and I love it.

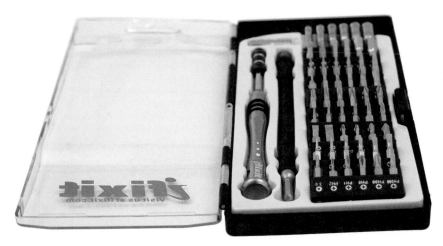

FIGURE 2.3   The iFixit 54-bit driver kit.

Spudger

A spudger (see Figure 2.4; a spudger is on the right) is an ESD-safe tool that is usually made of plastic or wood. You use it to poke, pry, and make adjustments to your iDevices or other small electronic components. You can also find metal spudgers, although I don't recommend them because of their ESD conductivity and tendency to scratch iDevice cases.

NOTE

A Little Etymology

In case any of you are word nerds like I am, the etymology of the word *spudger* is interesting. Spudger dates to approximately 1425–75, from the late Middle English noun *spuddle* ("short knife"). You learn something new every day, don't you?

Plastic Opening Tool(s)

Plastic opening tools (see Figure 2.4) provide a component-friendly, ESD-safe, disposable method for prying open iDevice cases and internal connectors. These tools are sold in a variety of sizes and are inexpensive (approximately $3.00 per pair).

FIGURE 2.4   The iPod opening tools are on the left, and the spudger is on the right.

You often see these implements called "iPod opening tools." However, these tools come in handy for opening and making adjustments to any iOS device.

It is worth noting that these tools degrade with use. Thus, you should ensure that you always have a healthy stockpile of opening tools in your tech toolkit.

Heat Gun/Hair Dryer

Really? I recommend that you purchase a heat gun or whip out your trusty hair dryer for iDevice repair? Well, as it happens, friends, a heat gun or hair dryer is invaluable for loosening the adhesive that binds together iPod and iPad cases.

The heat gun sold by iFixit, shown in Figure 2.5, produces 70°F at the low setting and up to 1112°F at the high setting. The take-home message is that you need to be careful not to overheat your iDevice cases so you don't melt anything!

TIP

Hair Dryers Are for...Hair

Frankly, using hair dryers for iDevice repair is a "hit or miss" operation because most consumer hair dryers might not provide the necessary amount of heat required to loosen iDevice case glue. Thus, your best bet is to invest in an honest-to-goodness heat gun.

CAUTION

I'm Melting!

It should go without saying, but my legal department insists that I point out that heat guns are very, very dangerous and can easily melt many items, including your flesh, your wife's curtains, the cat—anything that gets near the tool's business end. Heat guns are designed to make short work of melting heat-shrink tubing and the like, so they can make equally short work of melting other items you'd prefer not to have melted. You have been warned!

FIGURE 2.5   A heat gun—excellent for opening iDevice cases.

Magnetizer/Demagnetizer

A magnetizer/demagnetizer block (see Figure 2.6, left image) is one of those tools you didn't know you needed until you get one and think, "How could I have lived so long without one of these?"

You can use this tool to apply a low magnetic charge to your screwdriver bits. Trust me—this makes working with the iDevice's delicate screws so much more enjoyable and accurate.

As you would expect, you can remove the magnetization from your screwdrivers by passing them through the appropriate part of the block. This makes screwdriver storage less "sticky."

Pick-up Tools

The generic term "pick-up tools" refers to various tweezers, hemostats, clamps, and "doo-dads," both magnetized and non-magnetized, that are helpful for retrieving screws, plugging and unplugging connectors, and routing tiny wires (see Figure 2.6, tools on right).

FIGURE 2.6 A magnetizing/demagnetizing tool is on the left, and various pickup tools are on the right.

In contrast to the plastic opening tools, pickup tools are generally made of metal. Therefore, you should, in most cases, enjoy a long return on your investment on these implements.

Work Lamp with Magnifying Glass

You will thank me for suggesting that you purchase a goose-necked work light that has an integrated magnifying glass (see Figure 2.7, left image). Not only does this tool provide more light when you're working with iDevices, but it is also user friendly and gives you a fascinating close-up view of the microelectronics.

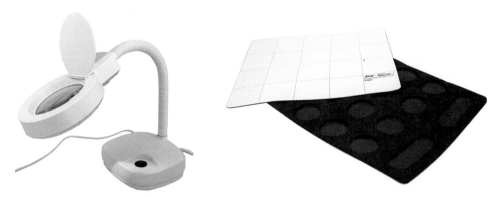

FIGURE 2.7   A work light is on the left, and magnetic project mats are on the right.

Magnetic Project Mat

Last, but not least, is the magnetic project mat. The one shown in Figure 2.7 (right image) comes from (you guessed it) iFixit, but you can feasibly make your own screw receptacle with resources as modest as a paper egg carton.

The bottom line is that you need a place not only to store screws and other tiny parts, but also to keep them organized in such a way that you always know which part/screw goes where in your device. Don't lure yourself into the cockiness of thinking, "Pshaw. I've field-stripped a dozen iPhones so far—I can do this stuff in my sleep." It is this reckless attitude that results in shoddy work, missing screws, and unhappy customers.

SO...DO I NEED TO SOLDER ANYTHING?

Understandably, some folks are put off entirely from the subject of electronics repair because they fear that they will be required to use a soldering iron. To be sure, soldering is an art unto itself, and a mistake with soldering equipment is likely irreversible.

By way of definition, *soldering* refers to permanently fusing two metal surfaces together by using a third metal called solder. Soldering requires burning-hot temperatures and a steady hand; unskilled individuals definitely can brick any electronics device by improper soldering.

The good news is that you are not required to use soldering to attach or detach components—unless you want to work on iPods. In iPhones and iPads, for the most part components are held together with adhesive, screws, and ribbon cables. Generally speaking, you are much better off completely replacing an iDevice logic board instead of taking your chances with a soldering gun, soldering braid, and oh-so-delicate circuit board components.

You'll discover soon enough that because Apple considers iPods (including touches) to be disposable equipment, they tend to solder internal components to the logic board. The take-home message here is that iPod repair is an approach that should be considered only by those with quite a bit of experience with soldering and desoldering.

Alrighty then! At this point you understand not only which character traits are required to be a good iDevice tech, but you have all the raw materials to equip a capable repair workbench. Now let's cover the pros and cons of industry certification.

Industry Certification

Apple offers a variety of certification programs that validate your expertise with either OS X information technology or creative applications such as Final Cut or the iLife application suite. Unfortunately, at this time Apple does not offer a certification credential for iDevice repair or support.

However, before I give you a blow-by-blow consideration of available certifications, you need to answer the fundamental question, "Why should I consider certification in the first place?" For certain individuals, certification is either required or, at the least, highly desirable.

Here are the main reasons why getting certified is a good idea:

- Increased professional credibility
- Gaining a leg up in the job market
- Meeting Apple's certification requirements
- Attaining deeper access to Apple tech resources
- Increased confidence

Let's consider each of these reasons in more detail.

Increased Professional Credibility

Adding an Apple certification logo to your resume or your business card lends a definite boost to your credibility. If you earn any certification, whether it is Apple or another certification vendor, you're telling prospective employers, colleagues, and clients, "I have invested time and effort to master this subject matter to the point where I have proved and documented my competency with an outside vendor."

Gaining a Leg Up in the Job Market

Let's face it: The information technology job market is booming, yet competitive. Whatever you can do to differentiate yourself from other candidates is a good thing. Speaking from my own experience as a hiring manager, if I were faced with two otherwise equally matched job candidates, in all likelihood I would take the certified individual before the non-certified individual. My thinking runs along the lines of, "This person went the extra step to document his or her competency with the subject matter. That speaks well of his or her character."

An additional benefit to Apple certification is that attaining the credential qualifies you for inclusion in the Apple Certified Professionals Registry (http://is.gd/mcYZtc). This is an online database of Apple certified individuals. Given how powerful social networking is in information technology, you might find that job prospects come to you as a result of your inclusion in this list!

Meeting Apple's Certification Requirements

According to Apple's own rules, all technicians who want to work for an authorized Apple repair center need to be certified. Because, as I mentioned earlier, there is not yet an iDevice-specific title, the certification you need is called the Apple Certified Macintosh Technician, or ACMT. I discuss the specifics of this credential later, but you should understand that if you don't work for an authorized Apple repair shop and still earn the ACMT, you aren't suddenly given Apple's blessings to perform your own warranty repair work. This is a quote from the ACMT home page (http://training.apple.com/certification/acmt):

> Please note that ACMT certification by itself does not authorize a technician to perform repairs on Apple products. Information on becoming authorized for servicing Apple products can be found at: http://apple.com/support/programs/

If you click that programs link, you go to the Apple Service Programs page, where you can learn about the institutional service options that are covered in Chapter 1:

- iOS Direct Service Program
- Self-Servicing Account Program (SSP)
- Apple Authorized Service Provider Program (AASP)

Attaining Deeper Access to Apple Tech Resources

If you earn the ACMT and are fortunate enough to score a job at an AASP or SSP, then you are privy to all sorts of wonderful Apple internal tools and diagnostics utilities. You also receive a login to the Apple Global Service Exchange (GSX) at https://gsx.apple.com. GSX is the interface between an Apple-authorized repair center and Apple itself. You can use GSX to access Apple's internal documentation library, place Original Equipment Manufacturer (OEM) parts orders, and use downloadable and online internal troubleshooting tools.

Increased Confidence

I humbly submit to you that after you exert the necessary blood, sweat, and tears to become certified by Apple or another certification provider, your morale should take a decided turn for the better. After all, you have documentary proof of your capabilities as an Apple technician.

Certification Options

The four Apple-related certification and para-certification programs I suggest for you are the following:

- Apple Certified Macintosh Technician (ACMT)
- iCracked iTech
- Apple Consultants Network (ACN)
- OnForce Consultant

Judging from the names in the list, you would be correct in assuming that the ACMT is an Apple title and the iTech is from a third-party certification vendor. To be sure, an Apple certification carries far more weight in industry than a third-party option such as the iCracked iTech. However, of the two programs only the iTech validates your skills with iOS devices specifically.

Apple Certified Macintosh Technician (ACMT)

This is how Apple describes the scope of the ACMT credential on the ACMT web page (http://training.apple.com/certification/acmt):

> *Apple Certified Macintosh Technician (ACMT) certification verifies the ability to perform basic troubleshooting and repair of both desktop and portable Macintosh systems, such as iMac and MacBook Pro.*

Of course, the kicker is the decided absence of any reference to iOS devices in that certification description. Thus, the ACMT certification deals with Apple desktop and portable systems only. To earn the ACMT, you must pass the following Apple exams:

- Mac Service Certification Exam (9L0-010)
- Mac OS X v10.7 Troubleshooting Exam (9L0-063)

Exam registration is $150 per attempt, and is scheduled through Prometric (http://is.gd/KCgZLQ).

By way of training resources, your best bet is probably the $300 AppleCare Technician Training (http://is.gd/AsKvTP). The license cost grants you one calendar year of access to a large library of self-paced training curricula, Apple service manuals, and documentation that is normally available only to AASPs and SSPs.

iCracked iTech

iCracked is a company that sells iDevice parts and repair tools; it also hosts a certification program called iTech. Although an iCracked certification has nowhere near the visibility or prestige as an Apple credential, you might be well served by pursuing the iTech title. Why? Let me tell you:

- **You receive focused training on iDevice troubleshooting and repair:** The folks in the iCracked network are working professionals who enjoy sharing knowledge. This means you can get a top-tier education in iDevice maintenance, even if it doesn't come from Apple.

- **You become part of the iCracked network:** This means that your contact information is available to potential customers in your geographical area. Therefore, you need to consider the iTech not only as a credential validating your skills, but also as a very real source of part-time or full-time income.

Essentially, iCracked serves as your broker. You pay iCracked a commission for each repair order that you receive from them.

If there is a "catch" to the iTech application process, it is the program cost. Should iCracked take you on as a certification candidate (and there is an extensive vetting process that consists of a written application, resume submission, and a telephone-based tech interview), you need to purchase a "Start-up kit" that runs upward of $700. Consider your options carefully—the "Start-up kit" doesn't guarantee you any customers, and all the information you need on device repair can be found either in this book, or on iFixit's website.

Hey, hey, hey—don't be alarmed. The contents of the kit are readily available (http://www.icracked.com/iTechs/more-details) and consist of nothing more than a suite of repair tools and an inventory of iDevice repair parts. It's actually a good requirement—you don't want to force your customers to wait on parts to arrive. Instead, you want to perform the repair and close the sale as quickly as possible.

OnForce Consultant

OnForce (http://www.onforce.com) is similar to iCracked inasmuch as it is a network of certified Apple professionals who pay OnForce a commission for work referrals.

The chief difference between iCracked and OnForce, however, is that OnForce is officially "blessed" by Apple Inc. Therefore, an OnForce consultant can receive referrals from local Apple Stores in the same manner as AASPs or ACN partners.

As you might surmise, this arrangement is controversial, with some AASPs and ACN partners complaining that Apple is robbing them of valuable referral business.

OnForce service professionals need to undertake a rigorous screening process to join. Your choice of information technology (IT) industry certifications varies depending upon the type of service you want to perform. Some of the certifications are associated with the following vendors:

- **Apple:** http://is.gd/opPeMy
- **CEDIA:** http://is.gd/733p4W
- **Cisco:** http://is.gd/dVmeZe
- **CompTIA:** http://is.gd/7gV6GB
- **Dell:** http://is.gd/NdHSFL
- **HP:** http://is.gd/pvgBCN
- **Microsoft:** http://is.gd/zc6iRj
- **Novell:** http://is.gd/coItdY
- **Samsung:** http://is.gd/ad7nAM

Apple Consultants Network (ACN)

If you are not affiliated with an Apple Store or an AASP but want Apple's permission to perform warranty repair work on iOS devices, then you should apply for membership in the ACN (http://consultants.apple.com).

The application process is time consuming, tedious, and costly, and you have to renew your membership each year. However, these annoyances are outweighed by the prestige of being an official Apple partner. Potential customers can easily find you by searching the Consultant Locator (http://consultants-locator.apple.com/). What's more is that you don't have to pay Apple a per-ticket commission like you do with OnForce or iCracked.

Is there a catch? Well, yes—isn't there always? You're fine with ACN if you want to do both business-to-business (B2B) and business-to-consumer (B2C) repair on Mac desktop and portable computers. However, if you want to specialize in iDevices then you must complete the additional requirements for the ACN Mobile Technical Competency (MTC; info at http://is.gd/YNCKtS) certification.

According to the ACN program literature, the Mobility specialization authorizes you to perform B2B-only service. Here's a direct quote from the source:

> *Install, integrate, manage, and support iOS devices in heterogeneous networks. You are able to successfully implement iOS devices in business environments. You are proficient in network integration, wireless technologies, network security, and device management. You are familiar with mobile apps and are looking to help customers discover innovative uses for mobile technology in their businesses.*

Note that there's a decided absence of anything related to iDevice repair. You will, however, be allowed to perform iDevice replacements. Fun, fun!

Protecting Your iDevice User Data and Settings

Have you ever brought in an iDevice (or a computer, for that matter) to a repair center for service? It is a vulnerable feeling, isn't it? After all, not everyone is as rigorous about backing up our data as you and I are. "What will happen to my stuff?" appears to be the most common fear of the customer.

As a Do-It-Yourself (DIY) iDevice technician you need to be ultra-mindful of the user's environment on their iDevices. In general, human beings detest change, and most iOS device users don't want anything to mess with their accustomed methods for getting from point A to point B on their devices.

This chapter describes the basic mechanics of iDevice backup and restoration. I cover only full-device restores in this chapter. Later in the book I explain how to selectively recover data from an iDevice. Let's get started!

What Exactly Do You Need to Back Up?

According to the Apple Support article "About iOS Backups" (https://support.apple.com/kb/HT4946), backups created with iTunes or iCloud include the following data from iPod touches, iPhones, and iPads:

- Purchased music
- Purchased TV shows
- Purchased iBooks books
- Purchased apps
- Photos and videos in the Camera Roll
- Device settings (Phone Favorites, Wallpaper, and Mail, Contacts, Calendar accounts)
- App data
- Home screen and app organization
- Messages (iMessage, SMS, and MMS)
- Ringtones

The basic guideline for iDevice backups is "if you bought it from Apple, it's backed up." If you delete an app from your iDevice, for instance, you can always freely re-download it from the Apple Store.

That said, you need to consider the data that is *not* included in an iTunes or iCloud backup. This data falls into the following two categories:

- eBooks that you sideloaded into iBooks
- Media (audio, video, and documents) that you added to your iTunes library manually

> **NOTE**
>
> **A Little Geekology**
>
> *Sideloading* refers to placing your own eBook content into iBooks or another eReader application. For instance, you can sideload eBooks formatted in the ePub or Adobe Portable Document Format (PDF) into the Apple iBooks app.

In order to protect your own iTunes library content on your iDevice, you must perform a synchronization (or sync) with iTunes, using either the USB cable or Wi-Fi.

Backing Up an iDevice by Using iTunes 11

In this book we assume that your iDevices run iOS 6 and that your PC or Mac runs iTunes 11. I understand that the 1st generation iPad can't run iOS 6, but I want these instructions to apply as universally as possible.

As you know, you can synchronize the content of your iDevice with iTunes software in one of two ways:

- Tethering with the USB cable
- Wi-Fi sync

Technically, synchronization and a backup are two different operations. However, the first step of an iTunes content synchronization is a backup. Synchronization pertains to your media libraries, which embraces your music, videos, podcasts, ringtones, and photos.

To perform a manual backup of your iDevice, ensure that the device is plugged in via the USB cable and appears in the iTunes device list. Next, perform the following steps:

1. In iTunes 11, make sure that you are in Library view as opposed to the iTunes Store view.

2. Select your iDevice using the top navigation bar.

3. On the **Summary page**, click **Back Up Now**. This is shown in Figure 3.1.

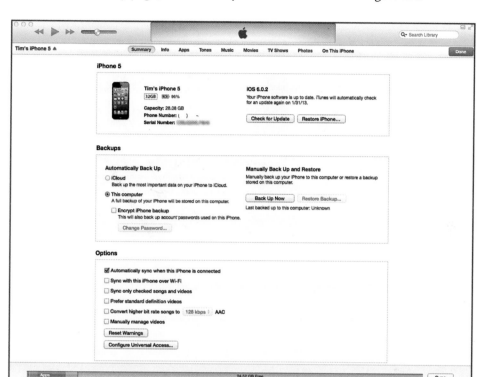

FIGURE 3.1   Performing a manual iDevice backup in iTunes.

TIP

Syncing Wirelessly

If your PC or Mac is on the same network as your iDevice then you can enable Wi-Fi sync and ditch the USB cable.

To set up your iDevice for Wi-Fi sync and backup, plug in your iDevice to your host computer, fire up iTunes, and perform the following steps:

1. In iTunes 11, navigate to your device as we described in the previous procedure. I've shown you the new iDevice navigation structure in iTunes 11 in Figure 3.2.

2. On the Summary page, select Sync with this <iDevice type> over Wi-Fi. You can see this option in Figure 3.1.

FIGURE 3.2 The new device navigation structure in iTunes 11.

Thereafter, you can initiate a manual Wi-Fi sync by navigating to Settings, General, iTunes Wi-Fi Sync on your iDevice and tapping Sync Now.

Where Are the Backup Files Stored?

You can review your iTunes-based backups directly from within iTunes. Follow these steps:

1. In iTunes 11, click iTunes > Preferences (OS X) or Control menu > Preferences (Windows). Incidentally, the "Control menu" in Windows is in the upper-left corner of the iTunes application window; yes, I realize that it is very difficult to find the menu intuitively.

2. In the Devices Preferences dialog box, navigate to Devices.

3. You can review all iDevice backups here. Hover your mouse over an entry to view metadata about your iDevice. The metadata includes your phone number, the IMEI, the MEID, and device serial number. This dialog box is shown in Figure 3.3.

If you are brave, you can also locate the compressed, encrypted iTunes backup archives on our host's computer's file system. The default backup location depends upon your operating system:

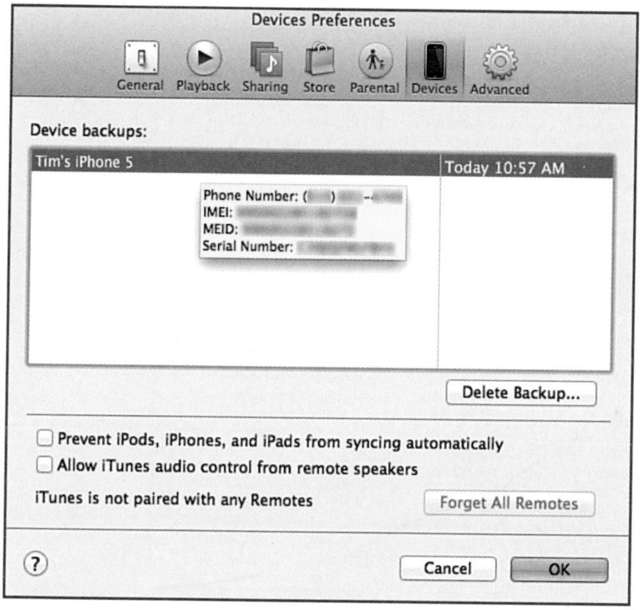

FIGURE 3.3   Metadata about your iDevice.

NOTE

Viewing Hidden Files

In both OS X and Windows, you need to configure the computer to show hidden files in order to view iTunes backup sets from within the OS X Finder or Windows Explorer, respectively.

- In OS X 10.7 Mountain Lion, iTunes backups are stored in ~/Library/Application Support/MobileSync/Backup. (Incidentally, the tilde [~] represents the currently logged-on user's home directory.)
- In Microsoft Windows 7 and Windows 8, iTunes backups are stored in \Users*username*\AppData\Roaming\Apple Computer\MobileSync\Backup.

Figure 3.4 shows the contents of an iTunes backup directory on an OS X host computer.

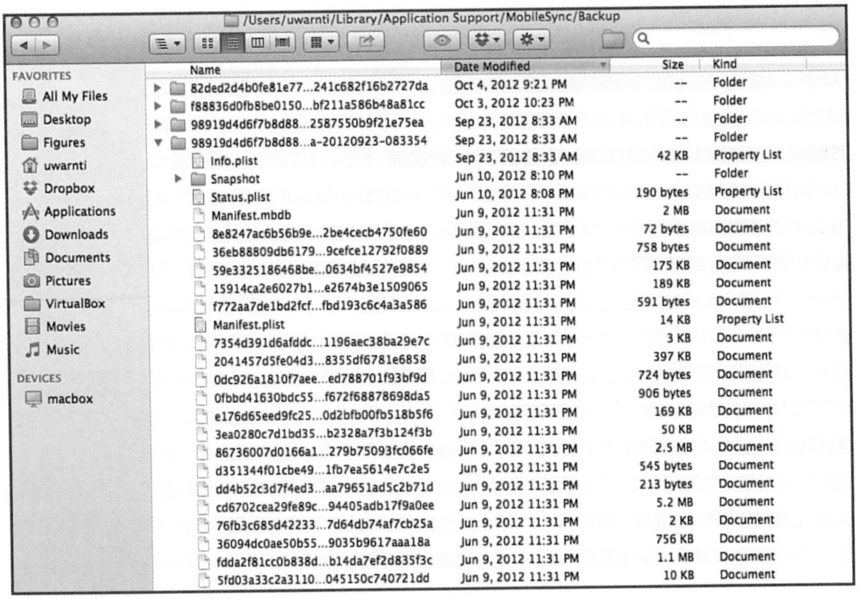

FIGURE 3.4   Contents of the iTunes backup folder on a Mac.

Observe that the raw backup files are named in an intentionally cryptic manner. Moreover, you can't simply delve into the backup archives from the host operating system and make much of any sense of their contents. For all intents and purposes, iTunes is your only practical method for leveraging these backup archives.

The good news is that you can back up these archives, move them to another host computer, and restore the data to your iDevice on that second computer. I cover that procedure in Chapter 18, "Recovering Data from Your Broken iDevice," which examines emergency data recovery.

Backing Up an iDevice by Using iCloud

iCloud is Apple's wonderful cloud-based storage and computing service. With iCloud you can transparently store your iDevice data on one of Apple's servers and almost completely break your connection to iTunes. (You still need iTunes to manage your media libraries, however).

To configure your iDevice to back up to iCloud, perform the following actions:

1. Using Figure 3.5 as your guide, simply select iCloud instead of This Computer for the Automatically Back Up option.

2. To initiate a manual backup, click Back Up Now.

NOTE

How Much Space Is Left?

iTunes 11 gives you a nice interactive graphic at the bottom of the iDevice Summary page that shows you how space is being consumed in your iDevice. Hover your mouse over a color-coded block to get the details. I show you this interface element in Figure 3.5.

FIGURE 3.5   Getting iDevice usage data from iTunes 11.

When you're set up with iCloud, your iDevice performs an automatic backup every 24 hours so long as your iDevice meets the following conditions:

- It's connected to Internet over Wi-Fi
- It's connected to a power source
- Its screen is locked

You can perform a manual iCloud backup of your iDevice by navigating to Settings, iCloud, Storage & Backup and tapping Back Up Now.

Backing Up an iDevice Manually

Historically, Apple has allowed an iDevice to synchronize with one and only one computer. If you, for instance, attempt to sync an iDevice with a second computer then you receive the scary message box shown in Figure 3.6.

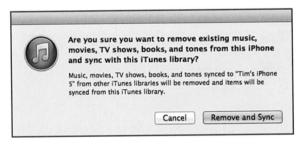

FIGURE 3.6 iTunes warning seen when you try to sync your iDevice with a second host computer.

If you proceed then the iDevice's content is wiped clean. This isn't desirable if, for example, you want to back up a customer's iDevice content (with their permission, of course) before undertaking repair work.

You can turn to third-party utilities that enable you to circumvent the one-computer limitation; I cover those tools in more detail in Chapter 18. At that time I also show you the mechanics of manual iDevice backup and restore.

In summary, if you have any choice in the matter, using iCloud or iTunes is by far the preferred way to back up your iDevice's data.

Restoring an iDevice by Using iTunes 11

The main problem with performing a full iDevice restore is the requirement that you be either within USB cable range or on the same Wi-Fi network as the PC or Mac with which you've synced the libraries.

Given that significant limitation, however, follow these steps to restore your iDevice by using iTunes:

1. In iTunes, navigate to the Summary page for your target iDevice.

2. In the Backups area, click Restore Backup.

3. In the Restore Backup dialog box, select your desired backup set from the drop-down list and click Restore. This dialog box is shown in Figure 3.7.

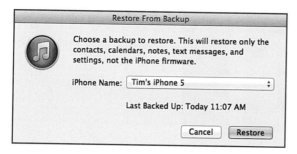

FIGURE 3.7   Restoring an iDevice by using iTunes.

Restoring an iDevice by Using iCloud

Speaking candidly (and have you known me to speak in any other way thus far in this book?), Apple has some work to do in terms of making iCloud-based restores more user friendly.

As it is, the only way to do an iCloud restore is to set up your iDevice as a brand-new device. Well, that works fine if you just purchased a new iPhone, iPad, or iPod touch. However, what if you need to reset your current device to its state as of its last iCloud backup? Here's the procedure:

1. On your iDevice, navigate to Settings, General, Reset, and tap Reset All Settings.

2. When the iDevice reboots, step through the configuration wizard. When you reach the Setup page, shown in Figure 3.8, be sure to specify Restore from iCloud Backup.

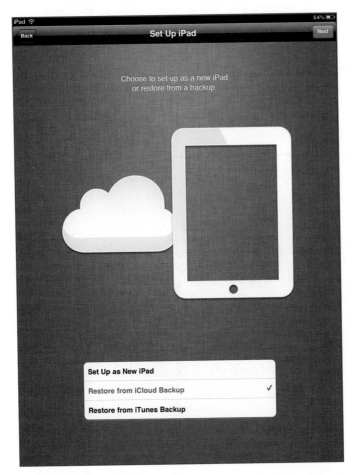

FIGURE 3.8 Restoring an iDevice from an iCloud backup.

Jailbreaking and Unlocking iDevices

To wrap up this chapter I'm briefly covering two popular iDevice hacks: jailbreaking and unlocking. Some newbies to Apple mobile devices confuse these two terms. They represent fundamentally different approaches to iDevice modification, although both of them enable you to customize an iDevice to meet your individual needs more closely.

What Is Jailbreaking?

In order to ensure a consistent user experience and minimize the possibility of a customer lousing up her iDevice, Apple configures its iOS operating system software in such a way that the customer never has full (root) access to the device.

Thus, *jailbreaking* refers to the application of code exploits that enable the user to circumvent Apple's built in firmware protections and gain root access to the iDevice's file system.

When iDevice enthusiasts released the first jailbreak exploits, Apple used legal means to fight back, citing intellectual property theft. However—and this is important—jailbreaking was upheld by a Digital Millennium Copyright Act (DMCA) exception ruling in 2010. Therefore, it is within your legal right to jailbreak your iDevice.

However—and this is equally important—Apple countered the DMCA ruling by stating that jailbreaking invalidates your Apple Hardware Warranty and AppleCare plan.

Here's the money quote from Apple Support Document HT3743 (https://support.apple. com/kb/ht3743; the emphasis in the following extract is mine):

> Apple strongly cautions against installing any software that hacks the iOS. It is also important to note that unauthorized modification of the iOS is a violation of the iPhone end-user license agreement and because of this, **Apple may deny service for an iPhone, iPad, or iPod touch that has installed any unauthorized software.**

The Apple Hardware Warranty has the following to say on the subject:

> This Warranty does not apply to an Apple Product that has been modified to alter functionality or capability without the written permission of Apple.

For completeness, the following extract is from the AppleCare+ Terms and Conditions contract:

> The Plan does not apply to an iPhone with a serial number that has been altered, defaced or removed, or has been modified to alter its functionality or capability without the written permission of the manufacturer.

Pros of Jailbreaking

All of this background information on jailbreaking is academic, however. The main advantages that jailbreaking your iOS device offers you are as follows:

- **You can install non-Apple Store apps:** As you may know, iOS apps must be submitted to Apple for approval before they are allowed to be listed and sold in the Apple Store. Thus, Apple has the final say whether such-and-so app becomes publicly available. By contrast, jailbroken iDevices can use Cydia, an alternative app storefront, to download and purchase apps that greatly expand the functionality of your iDevices (see Figure 3.9).

- **You can deeply personalize your iDevice:** Go to your local shopping mall and spend some time people-watching. You'll observe that it appears almost everyone using a smartphone is holding an iPhone—the devices are that popular. Without jailbreaking, the only way to personalize your iDevice is to purchase a custom case or cover.

FIGURE 3.9   The Cydia alternative app store for jailbroken iDevices.

Jailbreaking completely unlocks the firmware of your device such that you can dramatically change the device's look and feel. A good example of this customization lies in what is called *theming*, an example of which is shown in Figure 3.10.

■ The risk of bricking your iDevice is low: Perhaps the biggest fear people have of jailbreaking their iDevices is the idea that the process is irreversible (it is not), or that if something goes wrong their iDevices will be rendered permanently inoperable. I've been involved in jailbreaking since the iPhone 3GS, and I have never encountered a single case of a bricked iDevice. In a worst-case scenario, you have to perform a firmware and user data restore. I already covered the importance of regularly backing up your iDevice, so this fear is largely unfounded.

FIGURE 3.10   A heavily themed jailbroken iPhone.

"But what if I have to bring my jailbroken iDevice to the Apple Store for warranty service?" you might ask. "Will the tech at the Genius Bar be able to tell I've jailbroken the device?"

The answer to this question is simple: Your warranty repair should proceed just fine as long as you can restore the firmware of your iDevice prior to submitting the device to the Apple Store. The only problem you might encounter is if you show up at an Apple Store with a still-jailbroken device. In this case, you are almost guaranteed to be denied service.

Cons of Jailbreaking

The chief arguments against jailbreaking are relatively minor in impact, actually. Let's review them one at a time:

- **You will generally be required to lag behind in iOS version:** When Apple releases a new version of the iOS, it obviously takes the jailbreaking community a while to figure out a new way to exploit the operating system kernel code and render a safe and reliable jailbreak. In practice this means that most of the time you need to be content with running a slightly earlier version of the iOS that has a jailbreak developed for it.

- **Apple makes iOS downgrading very difficult:** Let's say you want to jailbreak your iPhone 4S that currently runs iOS 6. However, because an iOS 6 jailbreak isn't yet available, you decide to downgrade your firmware to iOS 5.1. Will this succeed? Yes, but only if you saved your Signature Hash (SHSH) blob from the previous iOS version. An SHSH blob is essentially an authorization ticket for a particular iOS version. Unless you use a third party app like Tiny Umbrella (http://thefirmwareumbrella.blogspot.com/) or Cydia (http://cydia.saurik.com/) to save your blobs, you won't be able to downgrade to an earlier iOS version; it's as simple and unfortunate as that. To further complicate things, Apple invalidates older SHSH blobs at an alarming rate, so in some cases even having a backed-up blob won't enable you to downgrade. Apple exerts tight control over its software as well as its hardware—has that fact been made abundantly clear to you yet?

- **You might be required to do tethered booting:** The two main types of iOS jailbreaks are tethered and non-tethered. Tethered jailbreaks require that you connect your iDevice to your host computer via USB cable in order to start up or reboot the device. This means that if you need to reboot your iDevice while you are on the road then you are out of luck. Naturally, the preferred jailbreak method is untethered, which means you can shut down and start up your iDevice any old time and retain the device's jailbroken status. In my experience, initial jailbreaks for a new iOS version are almost always tethered, which ties in to the aforementioned disadvantage of having to run an earlier iOS version to gain your freedom.

Unfortunately, we do not have the white space in this book to cover iOS jailbreaking in more detail. Instead, I recommend that you read the article series on the subject I put together for Que Publishing:

- "iOS Jailbreaking 101 Part 1: Understanding Jailbreaking" (http://is.gd/H5kcR7)
- "iOS Jailbreaking 101 Part 2: Ensuring Your Device's (and Your Data's)" Safety (http://is.gd/H0m6Mx)
- "iOS Jailbreaking 101 Part 3: Jailbreaking Your iOS Device" (http://is.gd/9IrpMy)
- "iOS Jailbreaking 101 Part 4: Making the Most of Your Jailbroken iOS Device" (http://is.gd/uQSz2h)

What Is Unlocking?

By default, iPhones are bound to a particular wireless carrier. You can visit the Apple website (https://support.apple.com/kb/HT1937) to obtain a comprehensive list of authorized cellular carriers. In the United States, AT&T, Verizon, and Sprint are the three main players in the mobile carrier service arena.

What this proprietary locking means for us, the customers, is that we cannot (again, by default) register an AT&T iPhone that is attached to the Global System for Mobile Communications (GSM) cellular network to another GSM provider such as T-Mobile. The same rule applies for Verizon or Sprint iPhones that employ the Code Division Multiple Access (CDMA) carrier network.

The good news is that both AT&T as well as Verizon offer authorized iPhone unlocking.

NOTE

Authorized Carriers

Please see Apple's list of authorized wireless carriers (https://support.apple.com/kb/ht1937) to see if your mobile carrier offers authorized unlocking.

The following is the basic procedure for performing an authorized unlock:

1. Ensure that your current wireless contract has expired (or you've paid your early termination fee).

2. Back up your iPhone.

3. Erase the contents of your iPhone.

4. Swap the old SIM card with the one for the new carrier.

5. Complete the iPhone Setup Assistant and restore your backup from iTunes or iCloud.

Incidentally, the Subscriber Identity Module (SIM) card lies at the heart of carrier unlocking. The SIM is a tiny integrated circuit (IC) module that (a) is tied to a particular wireless carrier and (b) contains your subscriber information and possibly your cell phone contacts list.

Specifically, this "subscriber information" consists of the following data elements:

- International Mobile Subscriber Identity (IMSI)
- Security authentication and ciphering data
- Carrier services to which the user has access
- Personal identification number (PIN)
- Contacts

You can see the AT&T SIM card from my iPhone 4S in Figure 3.11.

FIGURE 3.11   iPhone 4S SIM card and tray.

iDevice Repair Best Practices

This chapter takes care of some literal and figurative housecleaning that any self-respecting iDevice technician should undertake before performing any DIY work on iDevices.

I'm talking about answers to questions such as the following:

- How can I determine whether an iDevice is in or out of warranty?
- What do those strange acronyms like IMEI and ICCID mean?
- What's the difference between an iDevice Model Number and an Order Number?
- What do the strange hieroglyphics on the back of my iDevice represent?
- How can I maximize the safety effectiveness of my repair workshop?

Those are some juicy questions, don't you agree? What are you waiting for? Let's get to work!

Checking iDevice Warranty Coverage

Whenever you are presented with an iDevice and are asked to perform an out-of-warranty repair, the first thing you should do is definitively verify the actual warranty status of the device. Fortunately, you can easily find an answer to this question in ways that we will discuss now.

If you can't start the iDevice, then you can obtain the serial number, from the original product packaging or in iTunes. (You can find instructions for locating the serial number in iTunes in the sidebar later in this section.)

NOTE

Check the Back of the Device

Some older iDevice models have their serial numbers printed on the back case.

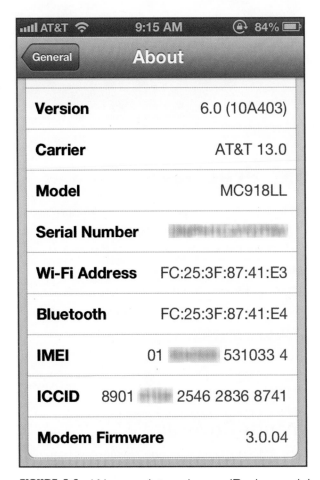

FIGURE 4.1 We can determine an iDevice serial number from within iOS.

You can check your iDevice serial number in iOS 6 by navigating to Settings, tapping General, and then tapping About. This interface is shown in Figure 4.1.

You can also submit the device's serial number to Apple's Check Your Service and Support Coverage page (https://is.gd/C8pEzh). The resulting web page, shown in Figure 4.2, provides you with the following information about the given device:

- Device purchase date
- Telephone technical support status, along with expiration date
- Repair and service coverage status, along with expiration date

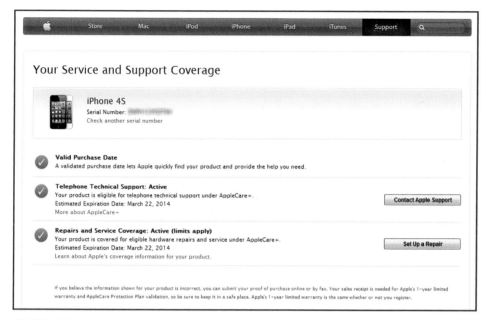

FIGURE 4.2   You can determine iDevice warranty coverage by visiting Apple's website.

FINDING THE SERIAL NUMBER IN ITUNES

Locating your iDevice serial number in iTunes 11 is easy. Plug in your iDevice and navigate to the device's **Summary** page in iTunes. The serial number is plainly displayed next to the small icon image of your device. Protip: Click the serial number value to toggle between the serial number and the unique identifier (UDID).

The format of the iDevice serial number is a combination of non-unique and unique information. It really does not behoove you to attempt deciphering Apple's serial number format because (surprise, surprise) Apple changes the format on a semiregular basis.

Instead, if you would like a breakdown of a given iDevice's serial number then I suggest that you visit the Dutch website Chipmunk International BV (http://is.gd/8BnvUi) or EveryMac.com (http://is.gd/wNrlgV). You can submit your device's serial number and obtain a list of detailed metadata concerning the origins of the device. This metadata includes the following:

- Year the model was introduced
- Production year
- Production week
- iDevice model name
- Order Number
- CPU speed
- Screen size
- Screen resolution
- Case color
- Capacity
- Factory of origin

To quote Miguel de Cervantes from his wonderful novel *Don Quixote*, "Forewarned, forearmed; to be prepared is half the victory." With that in mind, let's continue on the journey to iDevice metadata enlightenment.

Verifying iDevice Version Info

As you know, Apple has historically not been precise, much less consistent, in its product naming. For instance, consider the iPad. These are the official product names for the three generations of iPad:

- iPad
- iPad 2
- New iPad

Give me a break! What makes matters worse is that all three generations have simply **iPad** etched on the back panel.

The same goes for iPhones; remember our previous discussion of iPhone 3G, 3GS, and iPhone 4S? What relationship do those product names have with 3G or 4G carrier network connectivity? You have to consult a reference table to answer that question.

The most reliable method for identifying a particular iDevice model is to ascertain its model number. This alphanumeric string is printed on the rear case of the device (see Figure 4.3).

FIGURE 4.3   You can determine the iDevice model number and other metadata by viewing the rear case.

Use Table 4.1 as a reference to determine a model number.

TABLE 4.1   iDevice Model ID Reference Table

iDevice	Model ID
iPhone 3GS	A1303
iPhone 4 (GSM)	A1332
iPhone 4 (CDMA)	A1349
iPhone 4S	A1387
iPhone 5 (GSM)	A1428
iPhone 5 (GSM and CDMA)	A1429
iPad 1st generation Wi-Fi	A1219
iPad 1st generation Wi-Fi/3G	A1337
iPad 2nd generation Wi-Fi	A1395
iPad 2nd generation Wi-Fi/3G (AT&T)	A1396
iPad 2nd generation Wi-Fi/3G (Verizon)	A1397
iPad 3rd generation Wi-Fi	A1416
iPad 3rd generation Wi-Fi/4G (AT&T)	A1430
iPad 3rd generation Wi-Fi/4G (Verizon)	A1403

iPad 4th generation Wi-Fi	A1458
iPad 4th generation Wi-Fi/LTE (AT&T)	A1459
iPad 4th generation Wi-Fi/LTE (Verizon)	A1460
iPad mini Wi-Fi	A1432
iPad mini Wi-Fi/LTE (AT&T)	A1454
iPad mini Wi-Fi/LTE (Verizon)	A1455

What Are Order Numbers?

Order numbers are unique identifiers for iDevices that describe a unit's configuration, capacity, and color. These identifiers are alphanumeric strings that typically begin with MC or MD. For instance, the order number of one of my iPhone 4S devices is MC918LL. If you submit the order ID to a site such as EveryMac.com's Ultimate Lookup utility (http://is.gd/wNrlgV) you can learn the following about the device that has that ID:

- Specific date of manufacture
- RAM
- Storage capacity
- Model number
- Model ID
- Order number

You can obtain a comprehensive list of iDevice order numbers from various sources on the Web. For instance, try the iPhone Wiki's Models page at http://is.gd/QyN3Ox.

In contrast to the model number that is etched on the back case of your iDevice, you determine the order number from within iOS. Navigate to **S**ettings, General, About and scroll to the Model field. You can see this field in Figure 4.1.

Yes, yes, yes: We have hit a huge point of confusion here. Apple calls the order number by the term *Model* in iOS. No, you aren't crazy. This is one example of Apple's occasional (and frustrating) inconsistency within its iDevice family.

The reason I have spent so much time discussing iDevice identifiers is that most customers seem never to be quite sure that they have the iPad, iPod touch, or iPhone that they wanted. I can't say I blame them. After all, if I laid down $600 for a 3rd generation iPad then I want to ensure that I do indeed have the latest and the greatest model. From arm's length, the 2nd generation and 3rd generation iPads look virtually identical.

Deciphering iOS Speak

If you have spent some additional time nosing around the About screen in your iDevice's iOS or the home page in iTunes then you doubtless noticed some additional acronyms that may tickle your fancy.

- **The International Mobile Equipment Identity (IMEI)** is a globally unique identifier for GSM iPhones or iPads.
- **The Integrated Circuit Card Identifier (ICCID)** is a globally unique identifier for SIM cards.
- **The Electromagnetic Compatibility (EMC)** number is defined in electrical engineering (Reference: http://is.gd/e8JE43) as the "ability of electronic equipment to be a 'good electromagnetic neighbor': It neither causes, nor is susceptible to, electromagnetic interference (within the limits of applicable standards)."
- **The Integrated Circuit Card ID (ICCID)** is a yet another globally unique identifier associated with a GSM iDevice's SIM card. What's interesting is that you can run an ICCID through a mathematical formula in order to yield the subscriber's IMSI (International Mobile Subscriber Identity) number.
- **The Unique Device ID (UDID)** is a globally unique identifier associated with your iDevice that is used by iOS app developers to provision apps prior to their approval and availability at the Apple App Store.

As I mentioned in the earlier sidebar "Finding the Serial Number in iTunes," you can toggle through your iDevice's unique identifiers from within iTunes.

Okay, friends: Time for another experiment. Take your nearest iPhone, iPod touch, or iPad and turn it over. At this point you should feel proud of yourself inasmuch as you understand most of the information that is etched there.

However, the vast majority of iDevice users have no earthly idea what the collection of symbols (I affectionately refer to them as "hieroglyphics") means. Take another look at Figure 4.3 that shows an iDevice rear case and then read the meaning of each symbol, which is explained in the following list (working from left to right).

A: Approval seal of the US Federal Communications Commission (FCC). Note that the iPhone carries the FCC ID (grantee code) on the back case as well.

B: Compliance seal with the Waste Electrical and Electronic Equipment (WEEE) directive. This signifies that the iDevice can be disposed of in an environmentally responsible way.

C: Conformité Européene (CE) approval mark. This signifies that the device may be sold legally in the European Union (EU).

D: Refers to the body that approved the device for CE certification. 0682 refers to Cetecom ICT Services in Germany.

E: Alerts you of the iDevice's status as a Class II wireless device, which means that the iDevice may attempt to operate on wireless frequency bands that some countries disallow.

Whew—that was a heavy slog through acronymville, wasn't it? It's time to lighten things up by covering how warranty repair orders work for iDevices. Next we'll describe some aspects of an electrostatic discharge (ESD)-friendly workspace. After that I share some best practices, won through hard-earned experience, for organizing that workspace.

How Do Warranty Repair Orders Work?

I have to hand it to Apple in how they architected their Apple Retail Stores—it is a pretty slick operation.

Assume that your iPhone is malfunctioning somehow and you make an appointment to visit an Apple Genius at your local Genius bar by visiting the website at https://www.apple.com/retail/geniusbar/. What happens after you hand the Genius your iDevice?

1. The Genius uses Safari to access Apple's online iOS Diagnostics web app at https://iosdiags.apple.com. Apple Stores may alternatively use a hidden app on iOS devices called **iOS Diagnostics** or **Behavior Scan**.

2. The Genius opens a session ticket and sends a link to your iDevice.

3. After you agree to the process, the iOS Diagnostics web app runs a series of scans on your iDevice and generates a report.

The results of an iOS Diagnostics scan are pretty robust; they are generally broken into the following categories:

- Battery Health
- Usage Statistics
- Call Statistics
- Thermal Statistics
- Detailed Analysis

The "Detailed Analysis" also scrubs your iDevice for diagnostic log entries that may reveal the past installation of jailbreak apps. Remember that if the Apple Store technician discovers evidence of jailbreaking, your AppleCare warranty will be voided.

If, by contrast, the problem with your iDevice is definitely hardware-based, the Genius might (at the most) remove the bottom screws and remove the rear panel. You won't find that any Apple Store staffer field-strips your iDevice.

If your warranty claim is approved, you receive a replacement device–period. I sometimes wonder to myself if any Apple Store has an employee who knows how to completely disassemble an iDevice.

Apple Store personnel use a number of proprietary, internal iOS apps. It's far beyond our scope to consider these, but if you want to practice your Google-fu to learn more about them on your own, here is a not-at-all comprehensive list of internal app names:

- Apple Employee Directory
- AppleConnect
- Behavior Scan
- Chatterbox
- Concierge
- Espresso
- Merlin
- MobileGenius
- RFA
- speX
- Switchboard

Creating an ESD-Safe Workspace

Chapter 2, "The Tools of the Trade," covers the dangers of ESD. It also explains how you can protect yourself and your iDevice equipment against ESD by using an antistatic wrist strap and an ESD work mat.

At this time I'd like to share with you some additional tips and tricks to minimize the possibility of ESD causing damage to iDevice components.

Wear Appropriate Clothing and Protect Your Workspace

Please don't even think of wearing polyester clothing (such as a jogging suit) while you work on iDevices. Polyester is an absolute haven for ESD buildup.

Moreover, never introduce vinyl, Styrofoam, or plastic (except for your ESD-safe plastic work tools) into your workspace environment. Surely you've felt a static zap from vinyl, or had Styrofoam packing peanuts stick to your hands? These materials sound a potential death knell to IC components.

Believe it or not, you should strongly consider investing in ESD-safe, antistatic gloves. The reason for this suggestion is that the oils from your fingers can transfer all too easily to the tiny IC components and conductive contacts inside your iDevice. When this happens, you can unintentionally create extra resistance and potential short circuits. This is obviously not a desirable outcome, and it's difficult to troubleshoot these problems to boot.

ESD-safe gloves also carry the advantage of not leaving fingerprints on your pretty iDevice cases.

Handle IC Components Appropriately

Never place iDevice parts on a metal surface. Instead, place the parts on your antistatic work mat. For that matter, be sure that you have a supply of static-shielding storage bags on hand for easy parts transport. When you order an iDevice replacement part, the component should ship in a static-shielding bag. Don't throw them out! You'll be glad to have a stockpile of them on hand in your workspace for future use.

Handle all IC components only at their edges and never by their contact points. As I just mentioned, you need to ward against the transfer of your body oils to the contacts. You also don't want to create an inadvertent circuit bridge between the delicate contacts, which might very well short-circuit and fry them. It should go without saying, but here I go, saying it: Never touch another person who is working on IC components, and vice versa.

Condition the Air in Your Workspace

Industry best practice guidelines suggest that you keep the humidity of your workspace between 70 and 90 percent. You can achieve this level of humidity by measuring the humidity and then using a humidifier or dehumidifier in the room. Why leverage higher humidity? Because ESD charge levels are reduced (but not eliminated) in a higher-humidity environment.

You should also consider installing an ionized air generator in the room to add another layer of defense against the dreaded ESD.

Figure 4.4 shows a bench-top blower. Bench-top ionizers, such as the minIOS2 ionizing air blower (http://www.esdproducts.biz/Ionization/BenchtopIonizers/minION2/minion2.html) cost about $400. However, you must weigh this investment against the peace of mind of insuring against damaging iDevice components and risking dissatisfied customers who face unnecessary delays in parts shipments due to ESD damage.

FIGURE 4.4   A representative bench-top ionizing blower. (Image courtesy of Morn via a Creative Commons License: http://is.gd/tNxYFM)

Documenting and Securing Your iDevice Components

The worst-case scenario for any aspiring iDevice technician is to get well into a disassembly and having to ask, "Wait a minute. Which screws go with which part?" This is a rookie mistake that nearly all of us make in the beginning. However, you are reading this book to benefit from my experience. It is my sincere hope that you can skip merrily over many, if not most, of those beginner's pitfalls.

The very best screw and parts organizer I've ever used comes from our friends at iFixit. As you can see in Figure 4.5, the 8" × 12" magnetic work mat is divided into 20 squares on the magnetic side, and 16 cutout wells on the non-magnetic side.

FIGURE 4.5   iFixit magnetic work mats.

The idea is that you can use a dry-erase marker to number the magnetic squares, and for each step of a disassembly procedure you can store the associated screws and parts accordingly. The magnetism of the mat keeps those tiny screws in place.

The non-magnetic side creates an excellent organization space for larger, non-magnetic parts. Honestly, as an iDevice tech you will use the magnetic side of the work mat almost exclusively.

iPhone 3GS Disassembly and Reassembly

In many respects, using the iPhone 3GS as your first disassembly project is a great idea. The phone does not have as much "stuff" inside of it, for one. Another nice advantage is neither the battery nor any other internal components are soldered to the logic board (disassembling the iPod touch is an utter nightmare in this regard).

Finally, and I have no idea why Apple stopped doing this, the primary connectors inside the case are actually labeled, which assists in disassembly. Oh yeah—THAT'S why they stopped the practice.

Actually, I almost forgot what a blissful convenience it is that the display assembly for the 3GS pops off during the first couple steps of the disassembly. As you'll soon learn that replacing a display assembly for subsequent iPhones requires that you strip the dadgum device down to the chassis.

By way of trivia, you might have wondered what the S in iPhone 3GS (and iPhone 4S, for that matter) signifies. The generally accepted answer is that the S stands for *speed*. For proof of this, consider Table 5.1 that compares the CPU speed of the S and non-S iPhone models.

TABLE 5.1 iPhone CPU Speed Comparison

iPhone Model	CPU Speed
iPhone 3G	600MHz underclocked to 412MHz
iPhone 3GS	833MHz underclocked to 600MHz
iPhone 4	1GHz underclocked to 800MHz
iPhone 4S	Dual-core 1GHz underclocked to 800MHz

A Word About Underclocking

Apple configures iPhone Central Processing Units (CPUs) to run slower than they are capable in order to reduce the device's power consumption and heat emission, as well as to increase system stability. You might have also observed that the iPhone 4 and iPhone 4S have the same listed processor speeds and underclock ratios. However, the dual-core nature of the iPhone 4S A5 processor makes the 4S perform noticeably faster than the original iPhone 4, which sports the A4 processor.

Some Apple enthusiasts insist that the S stands for one of the following; I'll let you be the judge:

- Siri
- Slim
- Steve Jobs
- Same Design

The way I approach iDevice repairs is consistent for all hardware covered in this book. First, I review the iDevice's external anatomy. Second, I list the technician tools that are required to complete the disassembly. Third, I proceed through the disassembly step by step with lots of annotated pictures.

As you might (correctly) surmise, reassembly can be accomplished simply by following the disassembly steps in reverse order. However, with iDevice repairs and parts replacements there are almost always "gotchas" with reassembly. To that end, you'll find that I include a section called (appropriately enough) "Reassembly Notes" to assist you in that effort.

Now, without any further ado, I give you the iPhone 3GS!

iPhone 3GS External Anatomy

Headset Jack   SIM card tray   Sleep/Wake button

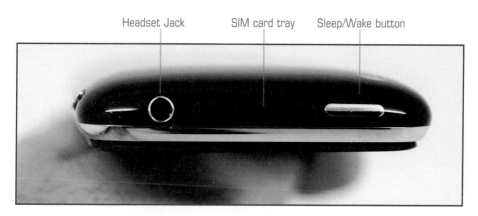

FIGURE 5.1   iPhone 3GS top view.

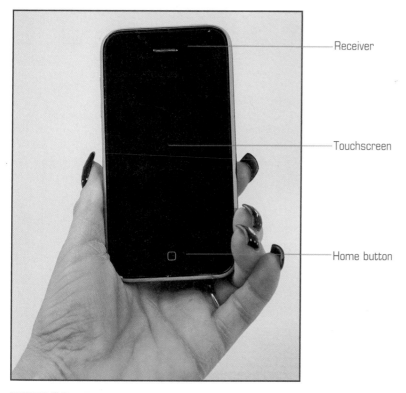

Receiver

Touchscreen

Home button

FIGURE 5.2   iPhone 3GS front view.

FIGURE 5.3   iPhone 3GS rear view.

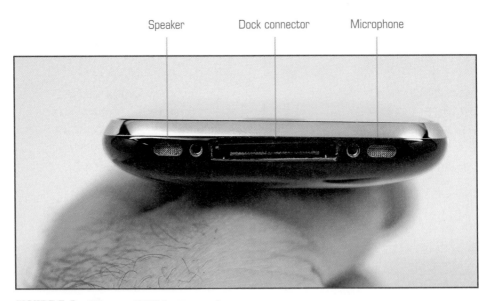

FIGURE 5.4   iPhone 3GS bottom view.

Disassembly Procedure

1. You use an iPhone SIM card eject tool or a paper clip to remove the SIM card tray from the iPhone. Insert the SIM card eject tool or paperclip into the hole located next to the headphone jack. Press down on the tool until the SIM card tray pops out (see Figure 5.5). You need to apply a fair amount of force to release the tray from the phone. At this point, if you want to remove the SIM card from the tray you may do so.

> **Required Tools**
> - Heat gun
> - Small suction cup
> - Phillips #00 screwdriver
> - Spudger

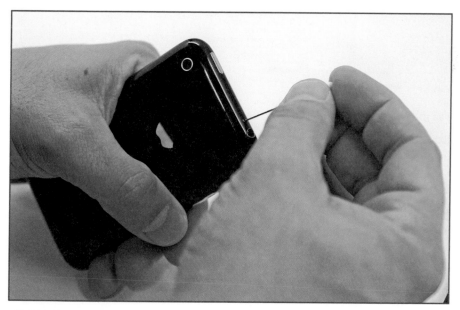

FIGURE 5.5   Removing the SIM card tray to access the SIM card.

2. Remove the two Phillips #00 screws located on the bottom (near the Dock connector) of the iPhone (see Figure 5.6).

NOTE

Be Gentle

Please be very gentle when you turn iDevice screws. If you use undue pressure, you'll strip the screw heads and render the screws worthless.

FIGURE 5.6 Removing the rear case screws.

3. Lay down the phone with its display glass facing down. Use the heat gun on the low setting to loosen the adhesive holding the display assembly to the chassis (see Figure 5.7). Be gentle with the heat, and never focus the heat directly on the glass.

4. Place a small suction cup directly above the Home button. Gently pull up the bottom portion of the display assembly but do not remove it just yet. Reminder: Do not yank the display assembly away from the rest of the case! There are three cables connecting the display assembly to the logic board. Instead, hold the display at a 45-degree angle from the rest of the unit (see Figure 5.8).

FIGURE 5.7 Heating up the iPhone 3GS to loosen adhesive.

FIGURE 5.8 Removing the display assembly.

CAUTION

No Yanking!

Do not yank the display assembly away from the rest of the case! There are three cables connecting the display assembly to that case. Instead, hold the display up at a 45-degree angle from the rest of the unit.

5. Use a spudger to carefully pry the ribbon cables labeled 1 and 2 from their respective sockets on the iPhone's logic board. The third ribbon cable labeled 3 is a ZIF (Zero Insertion Force) connector. Use the tip of a spudger to flip up the retaining flap on the third cable's ZIF socket. Make sure you are flipping up on the retaining flap and not the socket itself. Use the tip of the spudger to pull the third ribbon cable out of its socket. As we stated earlier, Apple helpfully labeled these connectors (see Figure 5.9).

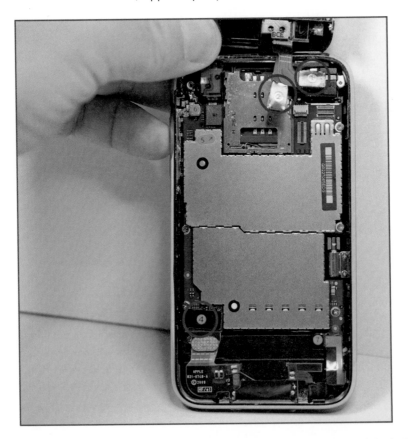

FIGURE 5.9 The iPhone 3GS display assembly has three labeled ribbon cable connectors. Cable #3 is located directly beneath Cable #2 in the image.

FIGURE 5.10   The proper method for removing a ribbon cable connector.

After you've removed the three ribbon cables (#1–#3), you can carefully remove the display assembly from the rest of the rear case.

6. Continue disconnecting the remaining ribbon cables (#4–#7) in the same manner as previously described. There is a hidden screw located under the Do Not Remove sticker. Make sure to carefully peel this sticker (peeling it most definitely voids your warranty). Remove the eight Phillips #00 screws securing the logic board and the rear-facing camera to the rear case that are shown in Figure 5.11. There are three different screw sizes; make sure to note the differences and keep track of them.

NOTE

Organization Will Set You Free

Now is a great time to make use of whatever method for organizing screws and parts you've decided upon.

FIGURE 5.11 Removing the iPhone 3GS logic board screws.

7. Use the flat end of a spudger to gently remove the rear-facing camera retaining clip (see Figure 5.12). Gently pry the camera out of its housing in the rear case. Do not remove the rear-facing camera. It is still connected to the logic board. The rear camera shoots at 3 megapixels (3MP) and also can do 30 frame-per-second (FPS) video at VGA (640×480) resolution.

8. Use the spudger to gently pry up the top edge of the logic board closest to the Dock connector. When it's loosened, you can slide the logic board toward the Dock connector and out of the iPhone (see Figure 5.13). At this point, if you want to disconnect the camera from the logic board you may do so freely by using the flat end of a spudger.

FIGURE 5.12   Prying but not removing the camera.

FIGURE 5.13   Removing the logic board.

NOTE

Those Apple Folks Are Clever

The two white paper dots on the EMI shield that covers the logic board are Liquid Contact Indicators (LCIs). All iDevices include several externally visible LCIs to help Apple Store Geniuses determine whether an iDevice has suffered water damage that would invalidate the warranty. I cover this subject thoroughly in Chapter 14, "Addressing Water Damage," later in this book.

MORE ON EMI SHIELDS AND LOGIC BOARDS

Apple makes extensive use of electromagnetic interference (EMI) shields in its iDevices. What is the importance of these metal covers? Well, the shields actually have a couple distinct reasons for being.

Primarily, EMI shields serve as a barrier between the logic board and other iDevice components. This barrier prevents electrical current from flowing between those components and thereby avoids electrical shorts.

Moreover, electromagnetic interference is simply a bad thing for portable electronics. The coupling of radio waves and/or electrostatic fields inside an iDevice results in signal reduction, which clearly is not desirable for the end user. Thus, you can clearly see the vital importance of these sheet metal shield components in isolating these various unseen forces from one another. The logic board is Apple's way of referring to the motherboard or main board of an iDevice. The logic board is truly the brains and heart behind the iDevice operation, and it consists of the following components (among many others, trust me):

- CPU (central processor) and GPU (graphics processor)
- Flash memory (permanent storage, analogous to a hard drive)
- Random Access Memory (RAM, temporary storage space that is cleared every time the device is powered off or restarted)

The logic board is also the central point of connectivity in an iDevice. In other words, all other components are somehow linked to the logic board.

What's important to note is that in iDevices the processor is not a monolithic unit. Instead, iDevice processors are as system-on-a-chip, or SoC, devices. The reason for this is that the SoC binds together most of the core functions of a computer motherboard (as shown in the previously given list) into a single, modular component.

9. To remove the Dock connector/speaker assembly, remove the three Phillips #00 screws; two on either side of the Dock connector and one near the #4 ribbon cable. Lift the Dock connector/speaker assembly out of the iPhone (see Figure 5.14).

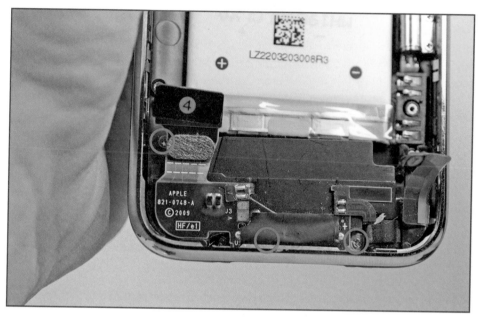

FIGURE 5.14   Removing the Dock connector/speaker assembly.

10. Use the spudger to gently pry the battery up from the iPhone 3GS's rear panel (see Figure 5.15). Apple stuck the battery to the inside of the rear case by using a mild adhesive. One idea you might want to consider is using the heat gun against the outside of the rear case to loosen the adhesive indirectly. If you do this, please be sure to use the lowest heat setting of your heat gun.

You know, it is truly a big deal that Apple decided not to solder the battery to the logic board. As I mentioned earlier, you'll see what a royal pain in the behind that is when you get to the iPod touch disassembly.

Figure 5.16 (courtesy of ifixit.com) shows the iPhone 3GS completely field stripped and laid out for the entire world to see.

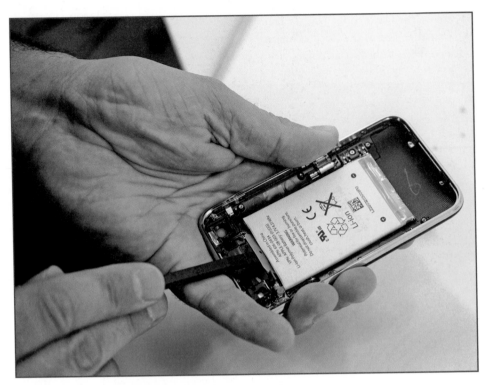

FIGURE 5.15 Removing the battery.

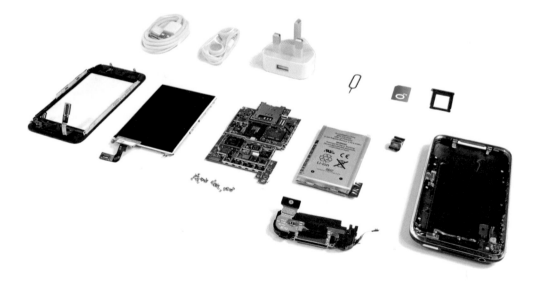

FIGURE 5.16 iPhone 3GS complete teardown. (Photo courtesy of ifixit.com)

Reassembly Notes

You might need to procure some adhesive or make use of 3M double-sided tape (http://is.gd/8hsZuc) to secure the battery (especially a replacement) to the interior of your iPhone 3GS.

Technically, any double-sided tape may work. However, I suggest the 3M type as it appears to be the standard that is used by iDevice techs.

Reconnecting the ribbon cable connectors is challenging at first. You have to exert quite a bit of force to get the connector to "stick." What makes matters worse is that you almost never hear the audible "snap" that ordinarily lets you know of a solid connection between cable end and logic board interface.

A Few Words About iOS 6

Believe it or not, you can install iOS 6 on an iPhone 3GS, but you cannot install iOS 6 on the 1st generation iPad. The reason for the iPad 1st gen not allowing iOS 6 probably has to do with its relatively light allotment of RAM (256 MB). Although the iPhone 3GS has the same amount of RAM and a similarly clocked processor, the iPhone 3GS needs to produce only 480×320 pixels on screen as compared to 1024×768 pixels for the iPad 1st gen.

At any rate, iOS 6 behaves surprisingly well on the now-ancient iPhone 3GS hardware. The biggest thing you will notice is that iDevice and iOS features that post-date the iPhone 3GS simply do not appear in the interface. I'm referring to things like fly-over 3-D maps in the Maps app, Panorama mode photos, FaceTime, and the like.

All in all, though, I suggest you stay with iOS 5.x if you plan to actually use the iPhone 3GS for any reason.

iPhone 4S Disassembly and Reassembly

If the iPhone 3GS represents the easiest take-apart in this book then I submit that the iPhone 4S is the most fun. What I think you'll discover when you disassemble the iPhone 4S is just how much "stuff" Apple was able to pack into a slim package. You'll be even more impressed by this space-consciousness when you take apart the iPhone 5 later in this book.

Before beginning the procedure, I thought it was apropos to briefly compare the iPhone 4 and the iPhone 4S in Table 6.1.

TABLE 6.1 Comparison Between iPhone 4 and iPhone 4S

Component/Aspect	iPhone 4	iPhone 4S
Weight	137g	140g
Processor	Apple A4 (single-core)	Apple A5 (dual-core)
Display	960×640 Retina	960×640 Retina
Rear Camera	5MP with flash	8MP with flash
Siri Voice Assistant	No	Yes
Carrier Speed	3G	4G

As you can see, the iPhone 4 and the iPhone 4S are virtually identical devices. Apple's big selling points for the 4S are that the 4S is faster (both in terms of carrier network speed and hardware performance) and has Siri (although the Siri aspect became less compelling with the release of iOS 6).

The inclusion of Siri in iOS 6 is a minor bone of contention with me, actually. The primary reason I upgraded from the iPhone 4 to the iPhone 4S was for Siri. My understanding at the time was that the 4S was the only iOS device capable of running Siri.

Of course, I (along with many other customers) fell victim to Apple's marketing spin. Oh, well.

External Anatomy

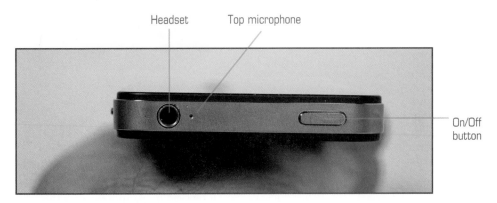

Headset   Top microphone

On/Off
button

FIGURE 6.1   iPhone 4S top view.

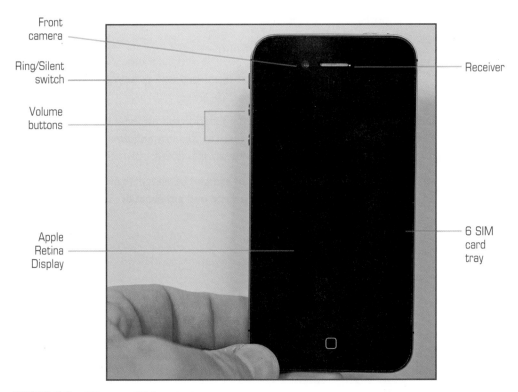

Front
camera

Ring/Silent
switch

Volume
buttons

Apple
Retina
Display

Receiver

6 SIM
card
tray

FIGURE 6.2   iPhone 4S front view.

Main camera

LED flash

iPhone

Designed by Apple in California. Assembled in China
Model A1387 EMC 2430 FCC ID: BCG-E2430A IC: 579C-E2430A

FIGURE 6.3 iPhone 4S rear view.

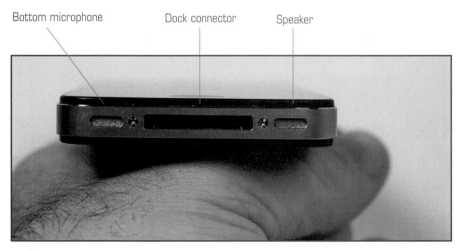

Bottom microphone   Dock connector   Speaker

FIGURE 6.4 iPhone 4S bottom view.

Required Tools

- Phillips #00 screwdriver
- Pentalobe screwdriver
- Tiny flathead screwdriver
- Plastic opening tools
- Tweezers

Frankly, this is a teardown that is made much easier if you purchase the screwdriver kit and plastic opening tools from iFixit prior to beginning the procedure. You can probably guess why Apple saw fit to use at least four different sizes of near-microscopic Phillips screws in the design of the iPhone 4S; namely to deter rogue repair techs from performing DIY procedures on iDevices.

The good news, however, is that I am able to take the phone apart just fine with the pentalobe, Phillips #00, and the tiniest flathead I have in my kit.

Without further ado, let's get started!

Disassembly Procedure

Use the following steps to disassemble an iPhone 4S:

1. Remove the two 3.6 mm pentalobe screws located on the bottom of the iPhone (see Figure 6.5). These screw heads are delicate; please be careful in your work so you don't strip the heads.

TIP

Penta-What?

In case you don't remember what the pentalobe screw is, I talked about it in Chapter 2, "The Tools of the Trade." The pentalobe is a custom screw head that Apple designed in an attempt to keep non-Apple techs from monkeying around inside the hardware. Beginning with the iPhone 4, Apple began using these custom-designed tamper-resistant screws to protect the outer case of iDevices. The first figure in Chapter 2 shows a close-up of this custom screw head.

2. After wrestling with opening the iPhone 3GS case, you will doubtless be surprised at how easy it is to remove the rear panel of the iPhone 4S. Simply use your thumbs to push the rear panel upward toward the top of the iPhone, as shown in Figure 6.6. The panel moves about 2mm or so. You can then lift the rear panel away from the rest of the iPhone.

FIGURE 6.5   Removing the two Pentalobe bottom screws.

FIGURE 6.6   Removing the iPhone 4S rear panel.

> **NOTE**
>
> **What is Aluminosilicate Glass?**
>
> The rear panel of the iPhone 4 and iPhone 4S is made of aluminosilicate glass; some of you might have learned this the hard way after dropping your iPhone and watching the spider web pattern appear. The iPhone 3GS has a plastic rear case and the iPhone 5 has an anodized aluminum rear case.
>
> Aluminosilicate glass, also sometimes called "gorilla glass," is made by Corning and is noted for its thinness, strength, and scratch resistance. This kind of glass is used in the windshield of high-speed trains and helicopters. According to Apple, alumino-silicate "is 20 times stiffer and 30 times harder than plastic." Although it's stronger than other kinds of glass, it still breaks and when it does, it does so in a spider web pattern, rather than shattering. Aluminosilicate is also sleek and very smooth, which makes for a nice feel in your hand and makes slipping the iPhone in and out of your pocket easier.

3. As you can see in Figure 6.7, the battery is secured in the case by means of a connector, which in turn is anchored by two slightly different-sized Phillips screws (1.5mm and 1.7mm). I was able to remove them both by using the Phillips #00 screwdriver.

FIGURE 6.7 Remove the two battery connector screws shown here.

4. Before prying the battery connector, use a plastic opening tool to pull the pressure contact from underneath the battery connector (see Figure 6.8). After the pressure contact has been removed, use a plastic opening tool to gently pry the battery connector from the logic board (see Figure 6.9).

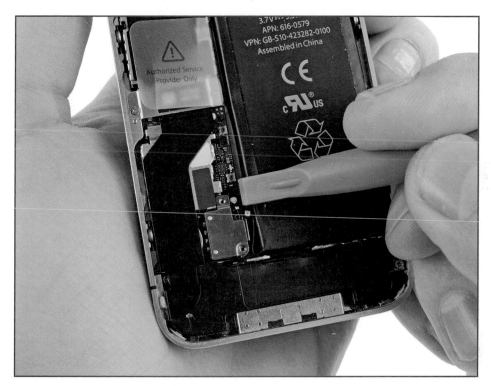

FIGURE 6.8   Pulling the pressure contact from underneath the battery connector. (Photo courtesy of ifixit.com.)

NOTE

Yet Another Word to the Wise

Be mindful to pry up the battery connector cable, not the logic board interface. Believe me—it's easy to make a mistake that will give you a lot of trouble to back out of with this kind of stuff.

FIGURE 6.9   Removing the battery connector.

5. The iPhone 4S battery is secured to the front of the iPhone 4S case by using (what else?) a mild adhesive. Use a plastic opening tool to gently pry up the battery along its right side. After you've loosened the battery, you can use the opposing pull tab to lift the battery out of the phone (see Figure 6.10).

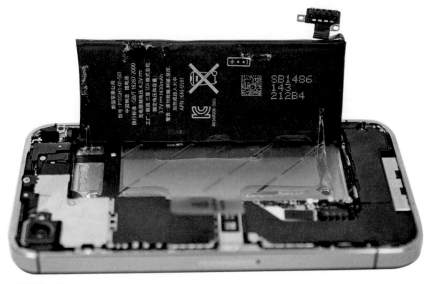

FIGURE 6.10   Removing the battery.

6. Now you disconnect the Dock connector cable from the logic board. To do this, you must first remove the Dock connector cable cover, which is held in by a 1.5mm Phillips screw and a 1.2mm Phillips screw (see Figure 6.11). Next, use the edge of plastic opening tool to pry the Dock connector cable from its socket on the logic board. Finally, carefully peel, but do not remove, the Dock connector cable from the logic board.

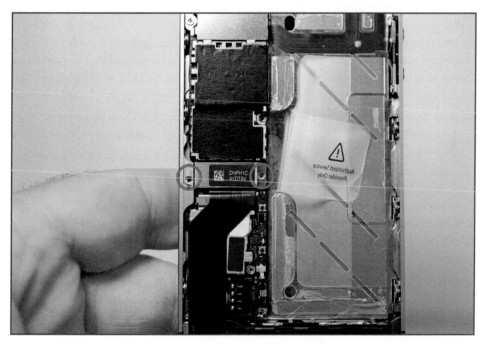

FIGURE 6.11   Disconnecting the Dock connector cable.

7. Now is as good a time as any to remove the SIM tray and SIM card. To do this, insert a SIM card eject tool or an unfolded paper clip into the SIM tray hole (see Figure 6.12). Moderate force is required to eject the SIM tray assembly.

8. Use the edge of a plastic opening tool to pry up the cellular antenna cable. Reroute the cable out of the way after you have separated the connector from its socket on the logic board (see Figure 6.13).

FIGURE 6.12 Removing the SIM tray and card tray.

FIGURE 6.13 Disconnecting the cellular antenna connector from the logic board. (Photo courtesy of ifixit.com.)

9. Remove the four Phillips screws securing the electromagnetic interference (EMI) shield/ cable cover to the logic board. These screws are circled in Figure 6.14.

FIGURE 6.14 Removing the screws that secure the metal cover over the logic board ribbon cables.

10. Use a plastic opening tool to pry the metal cover from the iPhone.

11. Take out the rear-facing camera next. First use a pair of tweezers to remove the outer plastic ring that lies on top of the flash assembly (as shown in Figure 6.15).

12. Second, use a plastic opening tool to pry the rear-facing camera connector from its socket on the logic board (see Figure 6.16). Lift and remove the rear-facing camera from the iPhone.

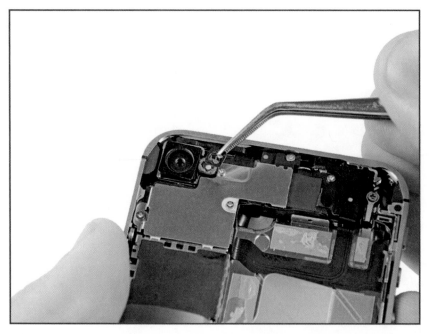

FIGURE 6.15 Removing the cover ring from the rear-facing camera. (Photo courtesy of ifixit.com.)

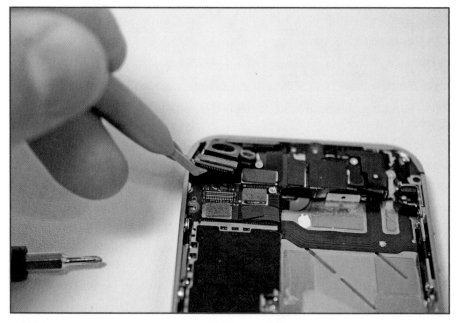

FIGURE 6.16 Removing the rear-facing camera.

CAUTION

Organization Will Set You Free

Removing the logic board from the iPhone 4S is much more difficult than it was with the iPhone 3GS. There are many screws that secure the logic board to the rest of the device, so make sure you stay organized!

13. Use a plastic opening tool to pry up the five primary logic board ribbon cable connectors; check out the annotated picture in Figure 6.17.

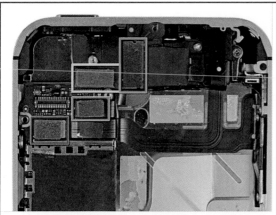
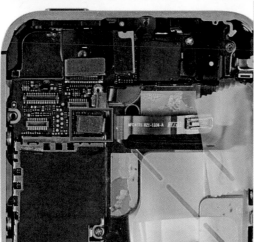

Step 18 — Logic Board

● Remove the five cables near the top of the logic board in the following order:

  ● Headphone jack/volume button cable
  ● Front facing camera cable
  ● Digitizer cable
  ● Display data cable
  ● Power button cable (located underneath the headphone jack/volume button cable as shown in the second picture.)

FIGURE 6.17 Detaching the primary logic board connector cables.

14. Remove the single 1.5mm Phillips screw that secures the grounding clip to the logic board near the headphone jack. You can then use a pair of tweezers to lift and remove the grounding clip as shown in Figure 6.18.

NOTE

Keep Your Eyes Peeled

Pay attention to where you place the grounding clip. It is a super-small, delicate part that is entirely too easy to lose track of.

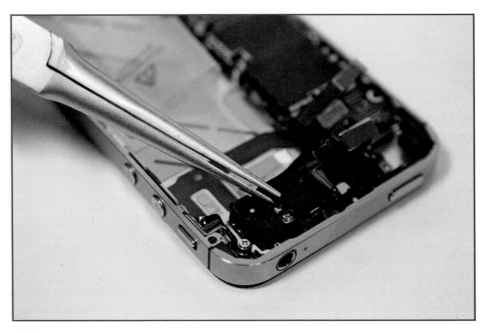

FIGURE 6.18 Removing the grounding clip.

15. Use your tiny flathead screwdriver to extract the 4.8mm logic board standoff, located near the headphone jack, shown in Figure 6.19.

16. Use the plastic opening tool to disconnect the Wi-Fi antenna (see Figure 6.20) from the logic board.

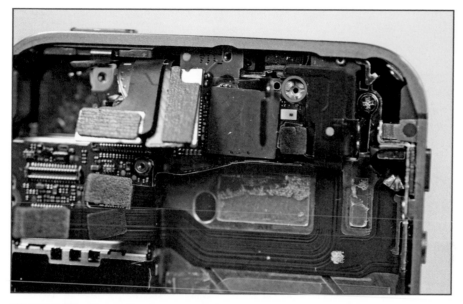

FIGURE 6.19   Removing the logic board standoff.

FIGURE 6.20   Disconnecting the Wi-Fi antenna.

17. Okay—time to get that logic board outta here. If present, carefully peel the piece of black tape covering the hidden 1.6mm Phillips screw located near the Power button. Use your tiny Phillips head screwdriver to remove the screw (see Figure 6.21).

In my experience, some iPhones have the hidden screw covered with the black tape, and some have uncovered screws. I tell you this so you won't be surprised when you open your iPhone 4S.

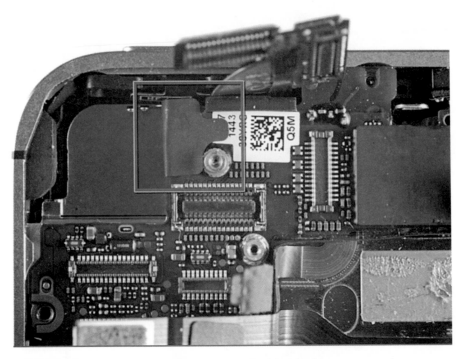

FIGURE 6.21 A hidden screw is covered with black tape.

> ## NOTE
>
> **Watch That Finger!**
>
> Please keep track of the delicate grounding finger for the rear-facing camera. It's a tiny component, and you need to make sure that it stays in place during reassembly.

18. Remove the final two Phillips screws that secure the logic board to the case assembly (see Figure 6.22). Use your tiny flathead screwdriver to extract the standoff located near the top of the speaker enclosure assembly.

19. Carefully lift the logic board out of the iPhone 4S as shown in Figure 6.23. Finally!

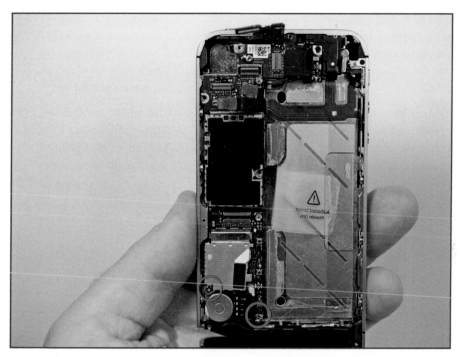

FIGURE 6.22 Preparing to free the logic board by removing the final two screws.

FIGURE 6.23 The iPhone 4S logic board.

20. Wedge your plastic opening tool between the vibrator and the side of the iPhone. Gently pry up the vibrator, as shown in Figure 6.24. The vibrator is held to the case assembly with adhesive.

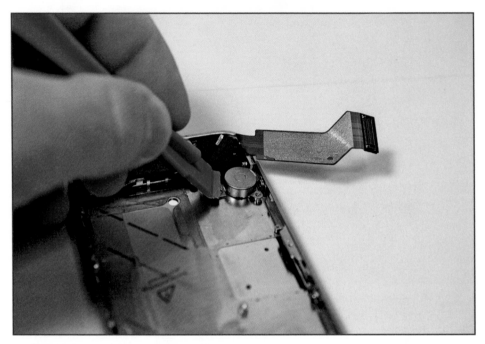

FIGURE 6.24   Removing the vibrator.

21. Remove the two 2.4mm Phillips screws to release the speaker enclosure assembly from the iPhone 4S. Use a pair of tweezers to carefully lift the speaker enclosure, as shown in Figure 6.25. This has to be one of the wackiest speaker enclosures I've ever seen in my life—what do you think?

22. The final step in this disassembly is removing the display assembly. To do this you need to locate and remove a substantial number of Phillips screws. If necessary, remove the small pieces of black tape covering the display mounting tabs. Next, remove the four Phillips screws underneath the display mounting tabs, each located in a corner of the iPhone. Finally, remove the six large-headed Phillips screws (three on each side) located along the inner perimeter of the case assembly. I've marked their locations in Figure 6.26.

FIGURE 6.25   Removing the speaker enclosure assembly.

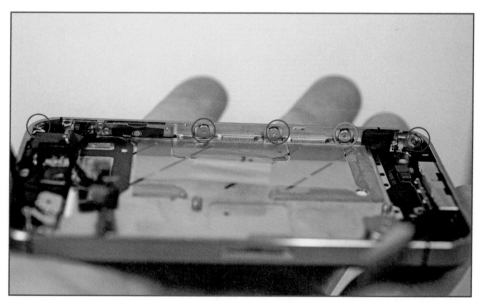

FIGURE 6.26   Preparing the screen assembly for removal.

Finally, use the edge of your plastic opening tool to gently pry up the display assembly around its perimeter from the rest of the case assembly (see Figure 6.27). Please remember that the glass, digitizer, and LCD are a single unit—don't try to separate those components!

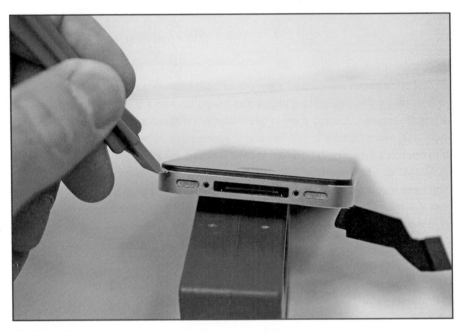

FIGURE 6.27   Removing the display assembly.

Figure 6.28 shows the completely torn-apart iPhone 4S.

FIGURE 6.28   iPhone 4S, completely disassembled. (Photo courtesy of ifixit.com.)

Reassembly Notes

- **Consider purchasing replacement screws**—The 3.6mm pentalobe screw heads are delicate and prone to stripping. Therefore, you should consider purchasing Phillips-style replacement screws from iFixit (http://is.gd/yVApxh) or another source.

- **Be patient with the cellular antenna**—Reattaching the cellular antenna connector tip takes an extraordinary amount of patience. As I told you in the iPhone 3GS teardown, there is no audible "pop" that lets you know the part is seated correctly. You have to use trial and error until the cable connector stays in place.

- **Keep track of those grounding fingers and EMI shields**—I made mention of this a couple times during the disassembly procedure, but it bears repeating: Make careful note of when and where you remove those tiny grounding fingers and mini EMI shields. Those are the most common parts to lose track of during an iDevice disassembly. However, Apple includes the parts for a reason, so you must be careful.

- **Windex makes a great lubricant**—Use Windex or a comparable glass cleaner to lubricate metal-on-metal contact points.

ON GLASS CLEANER AND RUBBER GLOVES

During your work with iDevice internals, the oils from your fingers can rub off on metal-to-metal contact points and produce electrical interference. In some cases the interference is such that it prevents the normal operation of the iDevice.

Note that I'm not talking about the copper contacts themselves; if you follow industry best practice, you never touch the contacts directly in any event. No, rather I speak of contact points between two metal components inside the iDevice.

There are two primary means of addressing the problem of errant skin oils:

- Rubbing the contact points with isopropyl alcohol or glass cleaner
- Using latex (or non-latex) gloves

Moisten a cotton swab or something similar with a glass cleaner or isopropyl alcohol and gently rub metal-to-metal contact points during your iDevice reassembly. Be sure to let the liquid dry completely before powering on the iDevice.

Of course, you can totally obviate the skin oil issue if you wear latex gloves. The downside to wearing gloves is that you will almost undoubtedly experience reduced manual dexterity.

Some iDevice Do-It-Yourself (DIY) repair enthusiasts recommend Nitrile gloves; these gloves are latex-free (good for people with latex allergies), powder-free, and are highly resistant to static electricity. Perform a Google, eBay, or Amazon search to find the best deal.

iPhone 5 Disassembly and Reassembly

The iPhone 5 is a work of beauty. Sure, the Lightning connector is a bit annoying until you have the appropriate adapters (or new accessories) in hand. Yes, the additional height of the device (the iPhone 5 is 8.6mm taller than the iPhone 4, and boasts a 4-inch Retina display) means you need a new case. However, in my experience, Apple did a phenomenal job on this phone. Beyond the pure aesthetics of the iPhone, the build quality is exceptional, and the performance is impressive.

The iPhone 5 is 1.7mm thinner and approximately 20 percent lighter than the iPhone 4—that is a substantial difference, no doubt due in part to the iPhone 5's anodized aluminum rear case compared to the iPhone 4's rear glass panel. The minimal actual glass in the iPhone 5 makes it not only much lighter, but less prone to breakage. Recall that front and/or rear glass breakage is by far the most common type of iPhone repair.

Benchmark studies demonstrate that the A6 processor outperforms the iPhone 4S processor by a margin of 150 percent. This is not surprising news, of course, because it is expected that each successive version of an iDevice will pack more horsepower than the previous editions.

One disappointment for me is that I was initially fooled into thinking that the set of perforations on the iPhone 5 bottom case meant that the it has stereo output. Alas, no: The Lightning assembly, which includes a bunch of other components within its mass besides the connector proper, sports only a single speaker. Bummer.

Another letdown regarding the Lightning connector assembly is that you will have to replace the entire thing if one of the individual components (for instance, the headphone jack) fails.

With respect to its reparability, the mechanism behind the display is stunning, and frankly surprising, coming from Apple. With nothing more than a suction cup and a Pentalobe driver, you can pop off the display assembly and swap it out with a replacement! That's right: You are no longer required to disassemble the iPhone to the bare metal to perform a display replacement. Awesome!

As of this writing, the iPhone 5's closest competitor is the Samsung Galaxy S III. Table 7.1 is a side-by-side comparison of the phones' major features.

TABLE 7.1 Comparison Between the iPhone 5 and Samsung Galaxy S III

Property	Apple iPhone 5	Samsung Galaxy S III
Release Date	September 21, 2012	May 29, 2012
OS	iOS 6	Android 4.0 (Ice Cream Sandwich)
Carriers	AT&T, Verizon, Sprint, regional providers	AT&T, Verizon, Sprint, T-Mobile, regional providers
CPU Speed	1.2GHz	1.4GHz
RAM	1GB	1GB
Display Resolution	1136×640	1280×720
Pixel Density	326	306
Diagonal Display	4"	4.8"
Rear Camera	8MP with 1080p video; LED flash	8MP with 1080p video; LED flash
Dimensions (in.)	4.87×2.31×0.3	5.26×2.78×0.34
Weight (oz)	3.95	4.69
List Price (16GB)	$199	$199

Speaking candidly, is it surprising to you that Apple sued Samsung for intellectual property (IP) patent infringement regarding the Galaxy S III smartphone's design? Sure, the Samsung handset was released three to four months before the iPhone 5. However, iPhone 5 specifications leaked to the Internet well before May 29, 2012.

Figures 7.1–7.4 show different views for the iPhone 5.

External Anatomy

NOTE

Bigger Is Better

The extra height of the iPhone 5 is such that users receive an additional row on their Home screens. All the more room to place more apps, right?

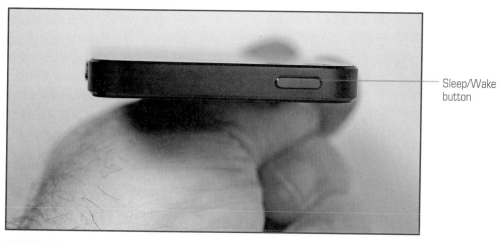

FIGURE 7.1 iPhone 5 top view.

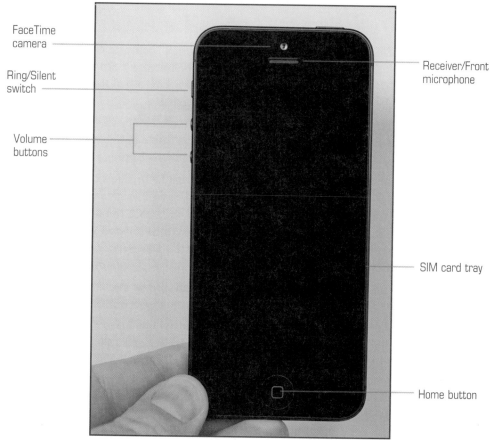

FIGURE 7.2 iPhone 5 front view.

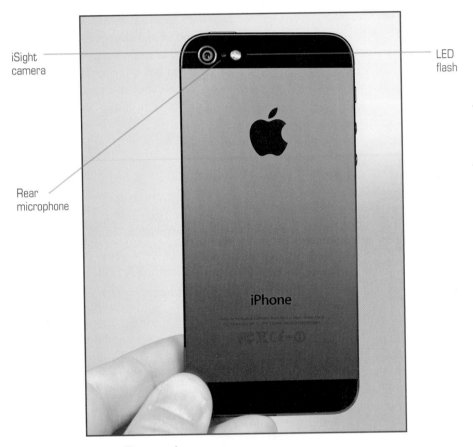

iSight
camera

LED
flash

Rear
microphone

FIGURE 7.3 iPhone 5 rear view.

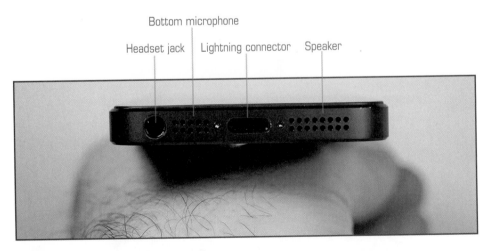

Bottom microphone

Headset jack | Lightning connector | Speaker

FIGURE 7.4 iPhone 5 bottom view.

Required Tools

- Screwdrivers (pentalobe, small flathead, Phillips #00)
- Plastic (and/or metal) opening tools
- Small suction cup
- SIM card eject tool
- Plastic (and/or metal) spudger

Disassembly Procedure

1. As you start the teardown, you'll see how easy it is to remove and potentially replace the front panel assembly. As previously discussed, Apple continues its trend of using proprietary, "tamper-resistant" pentalobe screws to hold the rear case together. Remove those screws, and remember to be gentle—you don't want to strip the heads (see Figure 7.5).

FIGURE 7.5   Removing the Pentalobe bottom screws.

2. Are you ready? Prepare to be utterly amazed. Attach your small suction cup to the lower portion of the iPhone 5 (just above the Home button). Hold down the iPhone with one hand. Lift up (with quite a bit of steady force) on the suction cup to create

a small opening between the front panel assembly and rear case. Wedge the edge of your plastic opening tool between the front panel assembly and the rear case and pry upward (see Figure 7.6). This should not be too difficult to do. Continue prying along the perimeter of the front panel assembly to release the clips securing the display assembly to the rear case. After the clips have been released, pull the front panel assembly away from the rear case (see Figure 7.7).

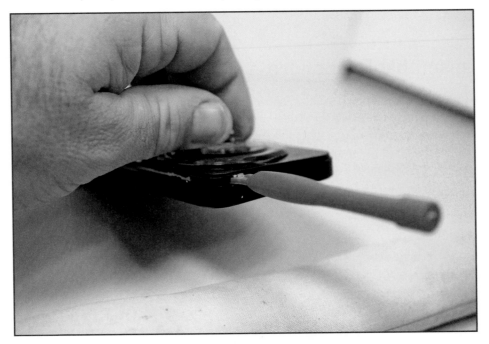

FIGURE 7.6   Prying up the iPhone 5 front panel assembly.

NOTE

Tale of the Tape

Be careful when you lift the front panel assembly because it still remains connected to the logic board by means of three tape-covered cable connectors.

3. Remove the three Phillips screws that secure the front panel assembly cable bracket to the logic board. Next, lift the bracket out of the iPhone (see Figure 7.8).

FIGURE 7.7 Lifting the iPhone 5 display.

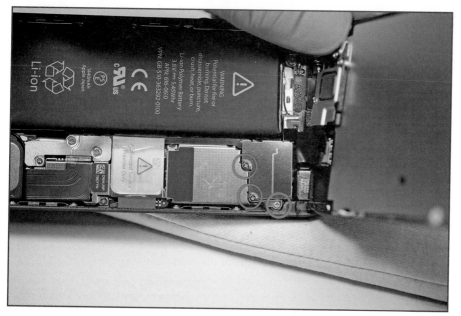

FIGURE 7.8 Removing the front panel assembly cable bracket.

4. Use your trusty plastic opening tool to disconnect the three front panel assembly cables. As shown in Figure 7.9, the three cables map to (1) the front-facing camera; (2) the digitizer cable; and (3) the LCD cable. Note that (3) is hidden in Figure 7.9; it is located beneath the digitizer cable.

> # NOTE
>
> **Leave Those Sockets Alone!**
>
> I know I sound like a broken record here, but please be sure to pry up only the connectors and not the sockets themselves.

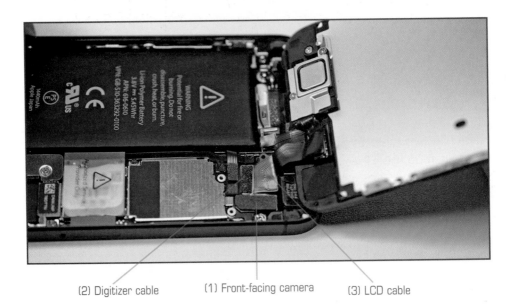

(2) Digitizer cable   (1) Front-facing camera   (3) LCD cable

FIGURE 7.9 Disconnecting the three front panel assembly cables.

5. Remove the front panel assembly from the rest of the iPhone. Lay the part aside and bask in how easy screen replacements are with the iPhone 5, especially compared to the same procedure with the iPhone 4S.

6. It's time to return your attention to the battery. The first task is removing power to it. Remove the two Phillips screws that hold down the metal battery connector bracket. (See Figure 7.10.)

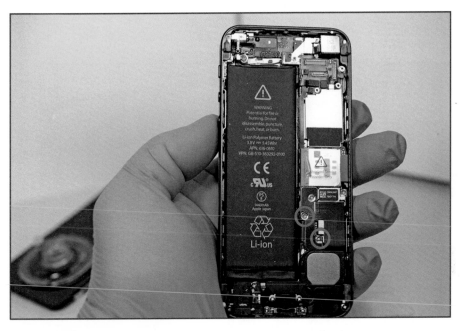

FIGURE 7.10 Remove these two screws to get at the battery connector.

7. Use your fingers (or better yet, a pair of tweezers) to remove the bracket as shown in Figure 7.11.

FIGURE 7.11 Removing the metal battery connector bracket.

8. Use your plastic opening tool to pry the battery connector from its socket on the logic board. (See Figure 7.12.) Leave the socket alone—you want only to lift the connector!

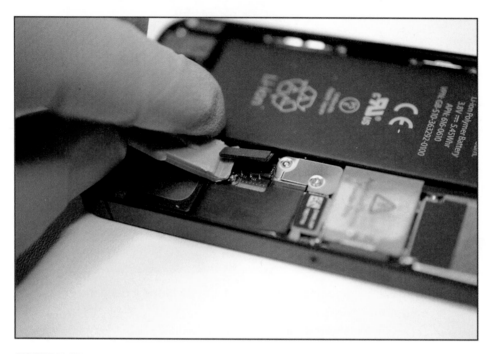

FIGURE 7.12   Disconnecting the iPhone 5 battery.

9. The battery inside the iPhone 5 is held to the rear case by a LOT of adhesive. Carefully but firmly run the plastic opening tool around the perimeter of the battery. Lift and remove the battery out of the iPhone 5, as shown in Figure 7.13. You may use the plastic pull tab to lift out the battery.

CAUTION

Assault and Battery

Be mindful not to puncture or grossly deform the battery. I say "grossly" deform because in my opinion the force that is required to unseat the battery from its adhesive will doubtless deform the battery package a little bit.

10. Use the tip of a spudger to disconnect the cellular data antenna cable connector from the logic board. The "button" connector is covered with a tiny square of felt. (See Figure 7.14.)

FIGURE 7.13 Removing the battery.

This tiny piece of felt covered
the button connector, but
was removed and set aside.

FIGURE 7.14 Disconnecting the cellular data antenna.

11. Remove the two Phillips screws (see Figure 7.15) and then use your fingers or tweezers to lift the top logic board bracket off the rear case. Take note of the component's orientation to make reassembly faster.

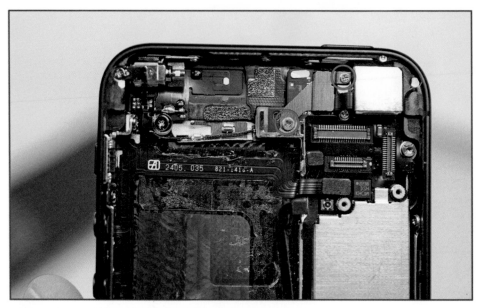

FIGURE 7.15 Removing the top logic board bracket.

12. Now you can work on disconnecting the myriad logic board cables. The iPhone 5 features two interconnect cables that use the same "button"-type connector head that you saw earlier with the cellular data antenna cable connector. (See Figure 7.16.)

13. Tilt the iPhone 5 chassis 90 degrees to reveal two additional Phillips screws as shown in Figure 7.17. Remove the two screws that hold the logic board to the rear case.

FIGURE 7.16   Disconnecting the primary logic board cables.

FIGURE 7.17   Removing two more screws that hold the logic board in place.

14. Remove the single Phillips screw that holds down the logic board bracket, and then use your fingers or a pair of tweezers to remove the mid-section logic board bracket itself, as shown in Figure 7.18. (Why do you think Apple includes so many of these metal-covering brackets in the iPhone 5? Do they serve a conductive purpose, a protective purpose, or both?)

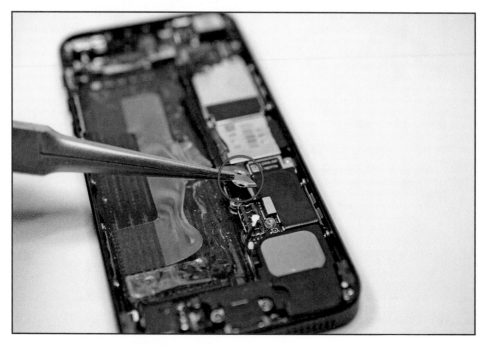

FIGURE 7.18   Removing the mid-section logic board bracket.

15. Whoops—you don't want to forget about the dadgum SIM card! Use a SIM card eject tool or a bent paper clip to eject the SIM card tray. You may remove the SIM card from the tray if you desire. (See Figure 7.19.)

FIGURE 7.19   Removing the SIM tray and SIM card from the iPhone 5.

16. You are almost ready to remove the logic board. First, remove the final set of five screws that secure the logic board to the rear case. As you can see in Figure 7.20, there are two types of screws at play here. The standoff screws are best approached with a small-gauge (2.5mm) flathead screwdriver.

FIGURE 7.20 Removing the Phillips and standoff screws that hold the logic board to the rear case.

17. Grasp the bottom portion of logic board and wiggle it to unseat it from the rear case. (See Figure 7.21.) Be mindful of the Wi-Fi antenna cable that is connected on the underside of the logic board.

18. Use the tip of the spudger to gently pry the Wi-Fi antenna cable connector from its socket located on the underside of the logic board. (See Figure 7.22.)

FIGURE 7.21   Removing the logic board.

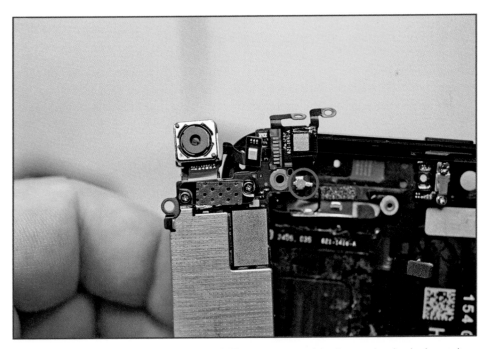

FIGURE 7.22   Disconnecting the Wi-Fi antenna cable from the logic board.

While you are here, take a look at the new Lightning connector assembly. A total of seven screws hold this monstrosity in place. (See Figure 7.23.)

FIGURE 7.23 The Lightning connector assembly.

What is important to note here is that this single, monolithic component contains not only the Lightning connector, but also the headphone jack and loudspeaker. This is bad news for us DIY'ers, as we need to purchase the entire assembly to replace an individual component.

Reassembly Notes

As I'm sure you observed, the interior of the iPhone 5 is filled with metal-to-metal contact points. Please keep in mind the best practices to avoid transferring finger oils to these components and creating unintentional electrical shorts and/or interference.

Don't worry too much if you need to deform the battery a bit during extraction. I was amazed at how much glue Apple used to secure it to the chassis. Simply flatten out the battery as best as you can prior to re-seating it in the rear case.

As discussed previously, the iPhone 5 includes a plethora of small metal connector brackets. Be sure to note their original orientation during disassembly to reduce or eliminate confusion during reassembly.

On Material Costs and Profit Margins

Market research companies like iSuppli (isuppli.com) take it upon themselves to disassemble electronic devices, source the vendor's cost for each and every component, and then compare the bill of materials (BOM) price to the unit's actual retail price.

According to iSuppli's September 18, 2012 press release (http://is.gd/KVvHoS), the iPhone 5 carries a $199 BOM. Stated simply, it costs Apple approximately $200 to produce an iPhone.

iSuppli tempers their data somewhat by stating that their iDevice disassemblies and cost estimates are "preliminary in nature, [and]account only for hardware and manufacturing costs and do not include other expenses such as software, licensing, royalties or other expenditures..." (source: http://is.gd/vXu2wp).

Now, compare that BOM figure with the list price for the 16GB iPhone 5 both with and without a cellular contract.

- Price without a contract (unlocked phone): $649
- Price with a contract: $199

Because you can reasonably assume that the vast majority of iPhone 5 customers buy the phone along with a contract (what good is a phone without a cellular provider, after all?), you must ask the question, "How does Apple make money if they break even on the iDevice cost?"

A ha...I'm glad you asked. Let's scratch the surface of this fascinating subject by listing a mere portion of Apple's myriad revenue streams for the iPhone 5:

- Apple charges accessory vendors a licensing fee.
- Apple earns a "cut" of every iOS app purchase in the Apple App Store.
- Apple earns a "cut" from every song, ringtone, audiobook, and so on sold in the iTunes Store.
- Apple makes money on its AppleCare warranty program.
- Apple sells its own accessories (Lightning adapters, for instance).

The aforementioned list is not comprehensive by any means. The bottom line is that Apple is able to offset the material cost of the iPhone 5's hardware by making a financial "killing" with related hardware, software, and license deals. The customer expenditures *surrounding* the iPhone 5's hardware seem to be where Apple derives its profit margin for this device.

Now don't you wish you owned a nice chunk of Apple stock?

iPad 2nd Generation Disassembly and Reassembly

The iPad 2 is a bit of an anomaly in the Apple iPad family. The 2nd generation iPad is thinner, lighter, and faster than the 1st generation model, but it does not sport the Retina display of the 3rd and 4th generations. The introduction of the 3rd gen iPad in March 2012 let us know that Apple planned a reliable yearly refresh cycle for the iPad platform.

But what happened? Spend a moment or two analyzing Table 8.1, which compares the different models.

TABLE 8.1 Comparison Among the Various Full-Sized iPad Models

iPad Model	Release Date	Discontinued?
1st generation	April 3, 2010	Yes
2nd generation (iPad 2)	March 11, 2011	No
3rd generation	March 16, 2012	Yes
4th generation	November 2, 2012	No

Not only did Apple release the 4th generation iPad a mere seven months after it gave us the 3rd gen model, but it also promptly discontinued the 3rd gen and retained the iPad 2! What's up with that?

Apple will never tell, but I have my suspicions. For my money, the biggest driver in Apple's decision to fast track the 4th gen iPad had to do with migrating the buying public to the new Lightning interface. We discuss the Lightning connector in great detail in Chapter 17, "Replacing the Logic Board and/or Dock Connector."

Furthermore, Apple has been tremendously obtuse in its iPad naming conventions (or lack thereof). The iPad 2 has a reasonable enough name. However, how can you quickly determine which iPad you are dealing with given the following official product names:

- 1st generation: iPad
- 2nd generation: iPad 2
- 3rd generation: The New iPad
- 4th generation: iPad with Retina Display

Crazy, isn't it? At least you can easily identify the 4th generation model by observing its anodized aluminum rear case and Lightning connector.

External Anatomy

Figures 8.1 through 8.4 show you the external structure of the 2nd generation iPad.

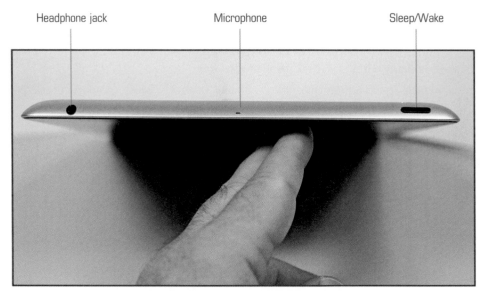

Headphone jack   Microphone   Sleep/Wake

FIGURE 8.1   iPad 2nd generation top view.

Front camera

Multi-Touch
screen

Home button

FIGURE 8.2   iPad 2nd generation front view.

Back camera

Side switch

Volume controls

FIGURE 8.3   iPad
2nd generation
rear view.

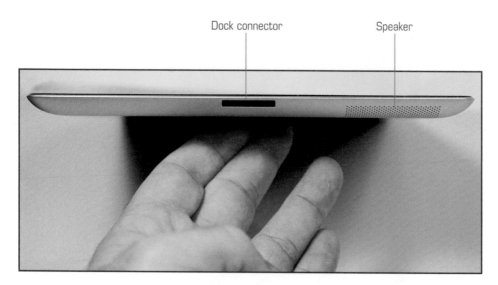

FIGURE 8.4 iPad 2nd generation bottom view.

The biggest news for you from a disassembly perspective is that, beginning with the iPad 2, Apple began affixing the front panel assembly to the rest of the case by using copious (and I do mean copious) amounts of adhesive. This is in stark contrast to the first generation iPad, whose front panel is attached to the rear case by easy-to-remove clips.

CAUTION

Buck Up, Campers

Speaking candidly, removing the front glass panel presents a near-insurmountable challenge for all but the most die-hard of DIY'ers. As I write this paragraph I have an iPad 2 next to me on my workbench with a completely demolished (think spider webbed) front glass. The gorilla glass is exceedingly unforgiving—if you apply just a smidge too much pressure, the display cracks and you need to order a replacement.

The ironic part is that after you've removed the front panel, the rest of the disassembly is easy. You will doubtless be impressed with how much empty space exists inside a full-sized iPad. The components that are present are arranged to make your access exceptionally easy and satisfying.

Required Tools

- Heat gun or iFixit iOpener
- iFixit "guitar picks" or general thin guitar picks
- Phillips #00 screwdriver
- Plastic and metal spudgers
- Metal and plastic opening tools
- Tweezers or needle-nose pliers
- Adhesive strips

Disassembly Procedure

1. As I mentioned earlier, I cannot overstate how difficult it is to remove the front panel assembly of the 2nd, 3rd, and 4th generation iPads.

2. Use the iOpener or a heat gun to loosen the adhesive as much as you can. Place the iOpener along the perimeter of the iPad's front panel for a few minutes. Remove the iOpener. Use a plastic opening tool to pry up the front glass from the black plastic bezel. Be sure you are wedging the opener tool between the glass and bezel and not between the bezel and the rear case—this is a common rookie mistake.

3. As you can see in Figure 8.5, you want to use one of your guitar picks to create an opening after you've cracked open the iPad just a tiny amount.

FIGURE 8.5   Using a guitar pick to shim the iPad 2 front display assembly.

4. As you pry up the front panel, watch out for "trouble spots." When you run your guitar pick around the perimeter of the iPad to break the adhesive, you need to pay attention to three special locations:

   ▪ Top center of the case (for iPads with carrier network capability)

   ▪ Bottom center/center right of the case (Wi-Fi antenna is located to the right of the Home button)

   ▪ Lower-left corner of the case (digitizer cable)

   I've called out these three trouble spots in Figure 8.6.

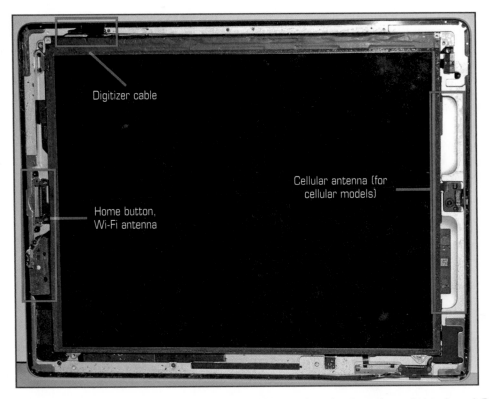

FIGURE 8.6 iPad display "trouble spots." Note also the location of the four LCD retaining screws.

5. When you lift the front panel assembly, flip it over and lay it to the immediate left of the iPad. The front panel is still connected to the rest of the iPad by the digitizer cable in the lower-left corner.

6. Take your trusty screwdriver in hand and remove the four Phillips screws to detach the LCD from the rear case. I've circled the locations of the screws in Figure 8.6. You can then carefully flip over the LCD and lay it down on top of the front glass assembly. At this point your iPad 2 is more or less an electronic "open book," both literally and figuratively speaking!

7. The digitizer ribbon cables don't have copper contacts; instead, they are held into two zero insertion force (ZIF) sockets by means of tiny retaining flaps. Use your plastic opening tool to lift the flaps as shown in Figure 8.7, and then carefully pull the digitizer cable out of the sockets. You need to peel back some black Kapton tape in the process as well.

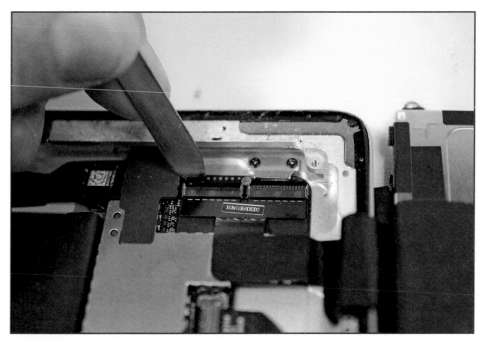

FIGURE 8.7 Detaching the digitizer cable.

8. After you've disconnected the digitizer cable, you can temporarily put the LCD back into the iPad 2. Carefully set the front panel assembly to the side. Our next task is to disconnect the LCD.

9. Use your plastic opening tool to lift the display data cable lock clip (see Figure 8.8). Next, pull the display data cable away from its socket.

10. You can now remove the LCD from the iPad. Set it aside.

FIGURE 8.8   Detaching the LCD data cable.

NOTE

Stop to Admire the Battery Cells

Spend a moment to take in the majesty of the triple battery cells inside the iPad. It's quite a wonder, isn't it? I discuss these Li-ion batteries in great detail in Chapter 16, "Replacing the Battery."

11. Use your trusty plastic opening tool to lift up the black piece of tape covering the end of the dock connector cable. Next, carefully pry up the edge of the dock connector's... well...cable connector (see Figure 8.9). You can then peel the connector ribbon cable partially off the rear panel.

12. By lifting up the dock connector cable, you have exposed the speaker cable connector. Use the plastic opening tool to carefully pry the connector upward (see Figure 8.10).

FIGURE 8.9   Detaching the Dock connector ribbon cable.

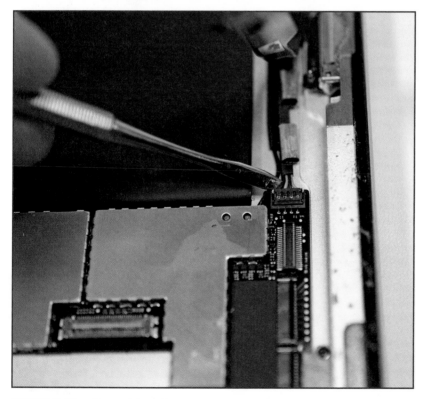

FIGURE 8.10   Detaching the speaker cable connector.

CAUTION

Patience, Grasshopper

Be mindful to pry up only the connector and not the socket itself when you remove any iDevice connector components. Be gentle and take your time!

13. There are still two cables attached to the logic board—the headphone jack/front camera cable and the control board cable. Use a plastic opening tool to flip up the retaining flap on the headphone jack/front camera cable ZIF socket. Peel the cable off the rear case, but do not remove it just yet. Pull the headphone jack/front camera cable straight out of its socket. In a similar manner, disconnect the control board cable connector from the logic board. Now, turn your attention to removing the logic board. Start by removing the two Phillips #00 screws holding down the logic board bracket (see Figure 8.11). Remove the logic board bracket. Next, remove the three Phillips #00 screws securing the other side of the logic board (see Figure 8.12).

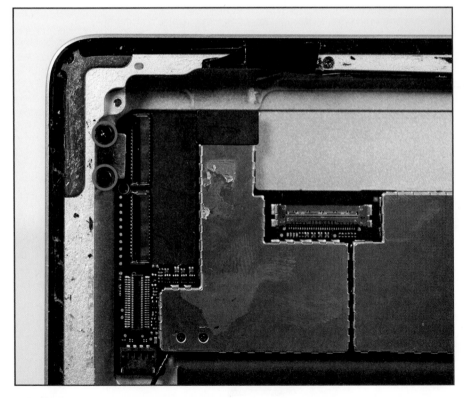

FIGURE 8.11 Removing the smaller logic board bracket.

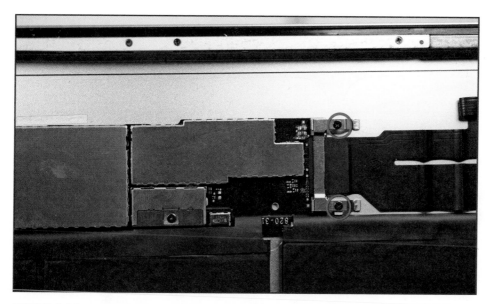

FIGURE 8.12   Removing the larger logic board bracket.

WHO KNEW?

The rest of the procedure, although easy, is nonetheless befuddling to me.
I must confess that in all my experience and research, I've never seen any acknowl-
edgement that the iPad 2 has (at least) two different connector structures for the
logic board. To illustrate my point, first take a look at the logic board connections
from iFixit's iPad 2 guide (http://is.gd/udjHJJ) shown in Figure 8.13.

Now, contrast what you just saw with the connector configuration on my own iPad 2,
which is shown in Figure 8.14.

Isn't that strange? iFixit refers to my iPad as the iPad 2.4, and it clearly represents
an unannounced revision to the iPad structure. iFixit is working on a guide for the iPad
2.4; be sure to re-visit iFixit.com regularly to check for updates.

Well, friends, this is my book so we are going to use my iPad.

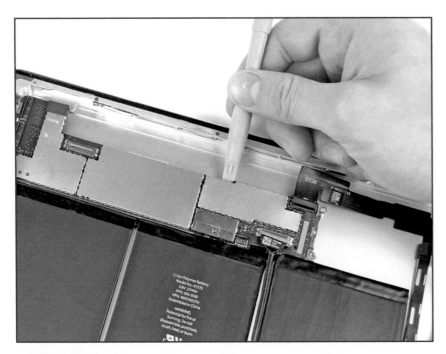

FIGURE 8.13   iFixit's perspective of the iPad 2 logic board connector cables. (Photo courtesy of ifixit.com.)

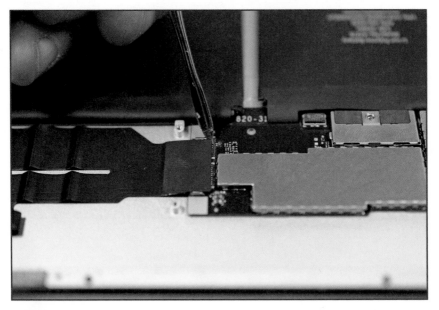

FIGURE 8.14   Tim's perspective of the iPad 2 logic board connector cables.

14. Use your plastic opening tool to remove the black tape covering the connector.

15. Use tweezers or needle-nose pliers to remove the data cable from its ZIF socket, as shown in Figure 8.15.

FIGURE 8.15 Disconnecting the logic board connector cables.

16. You can now wiggle the logic board out of the iPad's rear case (see Figure 8.16). However, don't yank out the logic board entirely! If you carefully flip the logic board over (the side nearest to the Home button) you will find the Wi-Fi antenna connector still attached (see Figure 8.17). You need to use a plastic opening tool to pry the Wi-Fi antenna connector.

FIGURE 8.16 Removing the iPad 2 logic board.

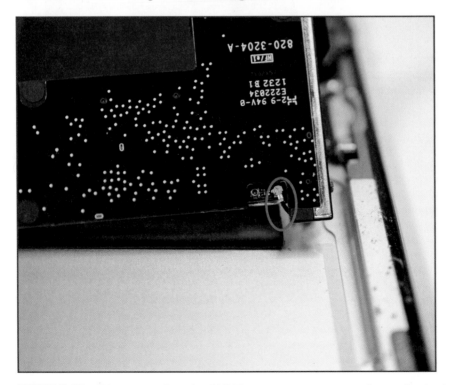

FIGURE 8.17 Disconnecting the Wi-Fi antenna connector from the logic board.

Reassembly Notes

To hedge your bet, you should obtain some adhesive strips to assist you in re-laying the front panel assembly back onto the rear case. Many iDevice technicians swear by the 3M 300LSE low surface energy adhesive transfer tape, but you can cut strips from just about any double-sided adhesive tape.

If you cracked the glass while taking apart your iPad (or if the screen was broken for some other reason), please take the time to remove every particle of glass from the chassis. I know that this seems like an obvious point, but in my experience it is sometimes the obvious points that get overlooked in the heat of the moment.

Consider wearing Nitrile gloves when you work to prevent the transmission of finger oils to metal components. Alternatively, use your tweezers or needle-nose pliers to hold components and wipe 'em off with a microfiber cloth.

Speaking of microfiber, make sure to wipe the LCD free of dust and fingerprints before you replace the front glass/digitizer. Believe me, you will regret it if you forget this step!

What Exactly Is a Retina Display?

Apple introduced its so-called "Retina display" in the iPhone 4S and the 3rd generation iPad. I'm including this discussion in this chapter because the Retina display is conspicuously absent in the iPad 2.

The first thing you need to understand is that "Retina" is an Apple marketing term and has no basis in industry standards. According to Apple, a Retina display packs picture elements (pixels, the smallest unit of a display) so tightly together that the human eye cannot discern individual pixels at a normal viewing distance.

Again, according to Apple, the threshold for human perception of individual pixels is a pixel density of approximately 300 pixels per inch. The iPhone 4S has a default pixel density of 326 pixels/inch. The 3rd generation iPad has a pixel density of 264 pixels/inch. However, the average viewing distance with the iPad is generally longer than that of the iPhone. Specifically, the average viewing distance for the iPhone is 10", compared to 15" for the iPad.

Screen resolution matters as well. Recall that the resolution of the iPhone 4S is 960×640, compared to 2048×1536 for the 4th generation iPad.

From a non-mathematical and eminently subjective human viewpoint, however, does the Retina display actually make a difference? In my humble opinion, I submit that it does. Try this experiment if you are fortunate enough to have access to a 3rd or 4th generation iPad as well as an iPad 2: Use the later gen iPad every day for a week and then abruptly switch over the iPad 2. If your experience mirrors mine, you will instantly (and unpleasantly) detect the pixelization of the iPad 2's display. It's quite noticeable. You'll find that the iPhone 3GS display (163 pixels/inch) is so blocky it's almost unusable.

As you learn in Chapter 10, "iPad mini Disassembly and Reassembly," the 1st generation iPad mini did not include Retina technology. This is surprising to me, but I'm sure it had to do with keeping the material cost as low as possible. It will be interesting to see if Apple incorporates Retina in the 2nd gen iPad mini. Many industry insiders find this prospect doubtful, because, to include Retina, Apple needs to boost battery capacity; this goes against the "mini" design spec of that iDevice.

9

iPad 3rd and 4th Generation Disassembly and Reassembly

In Chapter 8, "iPad 2nd Generation Disassembly and Reassembly," I told you that Apple replaced the iPad 3rd generation (called the "New iPad") with the iPad 4th generation (dubbed the "iPad with Retina Display") scant months after the 3rd gen's release. The first thing you should know is that the differences between the 3rd and 4th generation iPads are relatively slight. Thus, if you have a 3rd gen and felt cheated when Apple put out the 4th gen, *don't be.*

In my humble (or not-so-humble) opinion, the primary motivator for Apple to push out the 4th generation iPad was to standardize their mainline iOS devices on the Lightning connector. That's it. The notion is that as of Fall 2012, the iPhone 5, iPod nano 7th generation, and iPad 4th generation all share the same (new) connector. Big deal.

Besides the connector, Apple made the following incremental changes to the iPad 4th generation:

- **Processor:** The iPad 4th gen sports a 1.4GHz A6X dual-core processor, as compared to the 1GHz A5X dual-core processor that was included in the iPad 3rd generation.

- **FaceTime Camera:** The iPad 4th generation sports a 1.2 MP front-facing camera that captures 720p video as well. This is compared to the anemic 0.3 MP FaceTime camera on the iPad 3rd generation.

- **Carrier Network Capability:** The iPad 4th generation supports 4G LTE, whereas the iPad 3rd generation caps out at "standard" 4G.

If by contrast you are an iPad 2 owner, there are several very compelling reasons for you to upgrade to a 4th gen model, not the least of which is the crystal-clear Retina display. Table 9.1 details the major feature improvements between the two iPad models.

TABLE 9.1   Comparison of iPad 2 and iPad 4th Generation

Property	iPad 2	iPad 4th Generation
Release Date	March 11, 2011	November 2, 2012
Included iOS	iOS 4	iOS 6
CPU	1GHz dual-core A5	1.4GHz dual-core A6X
RAM	512MB	1GB
Display Resolution	1024×768 pixels	2048×1536 pixels
Pixel Density	132 pixels/in	264 pixels/in
Diagonal Display	9.7"	9.7"
Connector	30-pin	Lightning
Rear Camera	0.7 MP with 720p-quality video	5 MP with 1080p-quality video
Front Camera	0.3 MP with VGA-quality video	1.2 MP with 720p HD video
Dimensions (in.)	9.5"×7.31"×0.35" depth	9.5"×7.31"×0.37" depth
Weight (oz)	1.33 lb (Wi-Fi model)	1.44 lb (Wi-Fi model)
List Price (16 GB Wi-Fi model)	$399	$499

External Anatomy

Aside from the new connector (and model number; the iPad 3rd gen Wi-Fi model is A1416, and the iPad 4th gen Wi-Fi model is A1458), I defy anybody to differentiate these two iPad models by exterior examination alone. Figures 9.1 through 9.4 show the external anatomy.

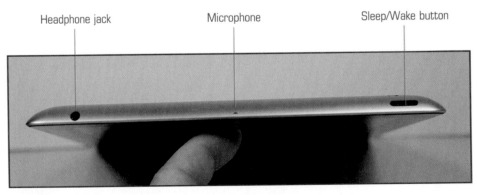

FIGURE 9.1   iPad 4th generation top view.

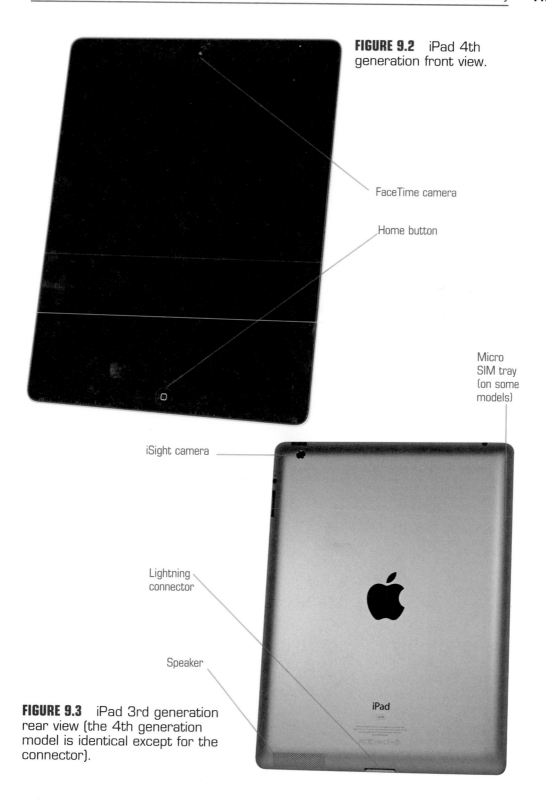

FIGURE 9.2   iPad 4th generation front view.

FaceTime camera

Home button

Micro SIM tray (on some models)

iSight camera

Lightning connector

Speaker

FIGURE 9.3   iPad 3rd generation rear view (the 4th generation model is identical except for the connector).

Figure 9.4 is particularly telling because it enables you to compare the 30-pin and Lightning connectors side-by-side (or one above the other, but you get the idea).

FIGURE 9.4 Connector comparison: 3rd gen iPad on top, and 4th gen iPad on bottom.

Required Tools

- iFixit iOpener or heat gun
- iFixit or standard thin-gauge guitar picks
- Phillips #0 and #00 screwdrivers
- Plastic and/or metal spudgers
- Plastic opening tools
- Adhesive strips

Disassembly Procedure

1. For detailed instructions on removing the front panel assembly from the 2nd-generation iPad, see Chapter 8. Unfortunately, the process for the 4th-gen iPad is every bit as troublesome and prone to shattering as it is with the iPad 2nd generation. The bottom line is that you need either a heat gun or an iFixit iOpener tool along with

several iFixit "guitar picks" and plastic opening tools in order to do the job, as shown in Figure 9.5.

FIGURE 9.5   Using iFixit tools to remove the front glass/digitizer assembly. The iOpener bean bag is at left, and the iFixit guitar picks are at right. (Photo courtesy of ifixit.com.)

Remember also the three main "trouble spots" of the iPad rear case where you need to be careful how you dig through the adhesive:

- **Top-center border of the case:** This is the cellular antenna (cellular models only).

- **Bottom of case, to the right of the Home button:** This is the Wi-Fi antenna assembly.

- **Bottom left of case:** This is the digitizer cable.

2. After you have the glass/digitizer assembly loose, you can flip it over like you are opening a book. Use your trusty screwdriver to remove the four Phillips #0 screws that hold the LCD to the rear case (see Figure 9.6).

   Use a plastic or metal spudger to lift and gently flip over the LCD such that it lies on top of the front display as shown in Figure 9.7.

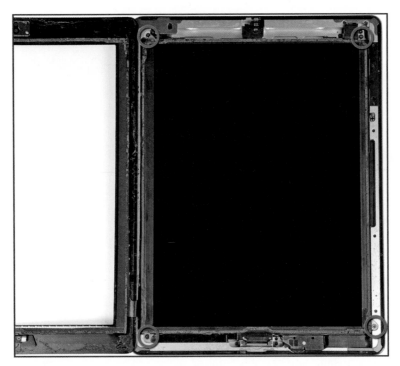

FIGURE 9.6 Removing the LCD screws. (Photo courtesy of ifixit.com.)

FIGURE 9.7 Rotating the LCD panel to expose the inside of the iPad 4th generation. (Photo courtesy of ifixit.com.)

3. There are three substeps to remove the LCD ribbon cable connector from the iPad 4th generation case:

    a. Use a spudger to peel back the piece of black tape that covers the LCD ribbon cable connector, as shown in Figure 9.8.

    b. Use the spudger to flip up the retaining clip of the zero insertion force (ZIF) connector.

    c. Use your fingers or a pair of tweezers to pull the LCD ribbon cable connector from its socket.

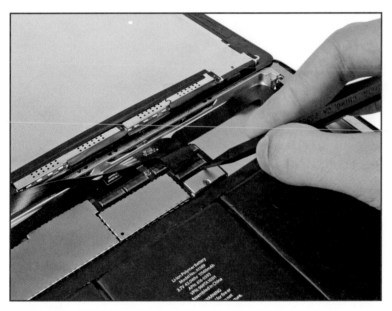

FIGURE 9.8 Disconnecting the LCD ribbon cable. (Photo courtesy of ifixit.com.)

4. Remove the LCD entirely from the rest of the iPad.

5. Turn your attention to disconnecting the digitizer ribbon cable from the logic board. Here are the three substeps:

    a. Use a spudger to peel back the piece of black tape that covers the digitizer ribbon cable, as shown in Figure 9.9.

    b. Use the spudger to flip up the retaining clips as you did for the LCD ribbon cable connector. Yes, there are two connectors, not one.

    c. Use the spudger or a pair of tweezers to pull the ribbon cables directly out of their respective ZIF sockets. You need to loosen some adhesive holding down the cable in the process.

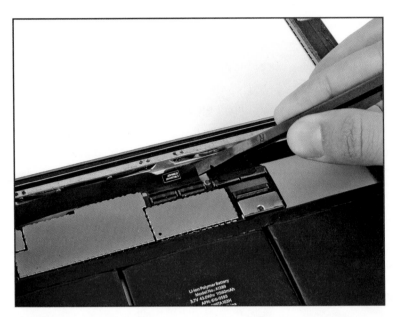

FIGURE 9.9 Preparing to remove the digitizer cable from the logic board. (Photo courtesy of ifixit.com.)

After you've pulled back the digitizer cable, releasing the adhesive along the way, you can lift the digitizer ribbon cable out of its recess from the rear case (see Figure 9.10). At this point you have the front panel assembly as well as the LCD completely detached.

6. Remove the piece of black tape covering three important logic board connectors:

   ■ **Wi-Fi antenna cable:** Use a spudger to detach this button connector. This part is called out in Figure 9.11 with a red box.

   ■ **Speaker connector cable:** Use the flat end of a spudger to pry this connector. This part is called out in Figure 9.11 with a orange box.

   ■ **Lightning/Dock connector cable** (depends on model, obviously): Use a plastic opening tool to pry up the connector. This part is called out in Figure 9.11 with a yellow box.

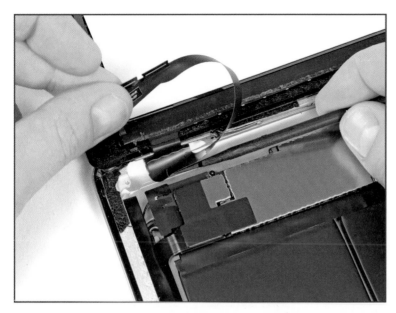

FIGURE 9.10   Removing the digitizer cable and freeing the front panel assembly from the chassis. (Photo courtesy of ifixit.com.)

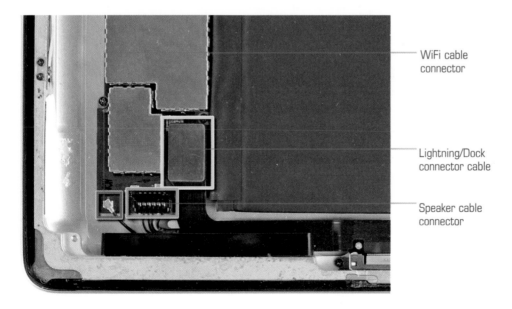

WiFi cable
connector

Lightning/Dock
connector cable

Speaker cable
connector

FIGURE 9.11   This is how the Wi-Fi antenna cable, speaker connector cable, and dock/Lightning connector attach to the logic board. (Photo courtesy of ifixit.com.)

7. You can remove the headphone jack cable the same way you approached the LCD and digitizer ribbon cable connectors:

   a. Remove the piece of tape covering the connector.

   b. Lift the ZIF retaining flaps.

   c. Remove the headphone jack ribbon cable as shown in Figure 9.12.

FIGURE 9.12   Detaching the headphone jack cable. (Photo courtesy of ifixit.com.)

8. Finish with the removal of the logic board. Use a #00 Phillips screwdriver to remove the four screws that secure the logic board to the rear case (see Figure 9.13).

9. Carefully grasp the edge of the logic board and gently wiggle to dislodge it from the rear case. Remove the logic board as shown in Figure 9.14.

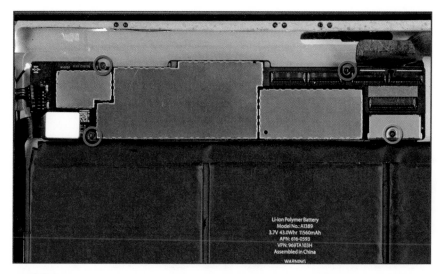

FIGURE 9.13   Removing the final four logic board screws. (Photo courtesy of ifixit.com.)

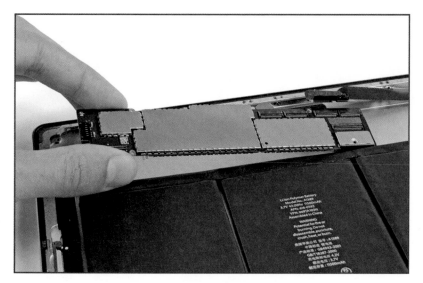

FIGURE 9.14   Removing the logic board. (Photo courtesy of ifixit.com.)

10. Removing the Lightning connector is a snap. Well, it's a couple of screws (see Figure 9.15). It's truly awesome that the Lightning connector in the iPad 4th generation is not soldered to the logic board (see Figure 9.16). As you see in Chapter 10, "iPad mini Disassembly and Reassembly," removing a Lightning connector is not always so easy.

FIGURE 9.15 Removing the two screws that hold the Lightning connector in place. (Photo courtesy of ifixit.com.)

FIGURE 9.16 Because the Lightning connector is an easily removable part, replacing it does not require replacing the logic board. (Photo courtesy of ifixit.com.)

11. Figure 9.17 shows the iPad 4th generation in its fully blown-out glory.

FIGURE 9.17 The 4th generation iPad, completely disassembled. (Photo courtesy of ifixit.com.)

Reassembly Notes

- You need adhesive strips to reattach the front display with any degree of security.
- The battery cells are glued into the chassis extraordinarily tightly. Therefore, although removal of the battery cells proves to be a significant challenge, reseating them is relatively easy because there is so much glue left over.

Why Do Front and Rear Cameras Have Different Resolutions?

As you know, Apple phones starting with iPhone 4 and tablets starting with iPad 2 include two cameras. Apple calls the rear-facing cameras iSight and the front-facing cameras FaceTime (see Figure 9.18). These terms are intentionally applied, for iSight is the name of Apple's internal and external webcam platform, and FaceTime is the name of Apple's video chat application and related protocol.

FIGURE 9.18 iPad 4th generation FaceTime camera.

As you can see by studying Table 9.2, the front and rear cameras in iPhones and iPads have different properties. Why do you think that this is the case?

TABLE 9.2 Comparison of iPhone 5 and iPad 4th Generation On-Board Cameras

Property	iPhone 5	iPad 4th Generation
Rear Camera Resolution (Stills)	8 MP with LED flash	5 MP (no flash)
Rear Camera (Video)	1080p HD at 30 frames/second	1080p HD at 30 frames/second
Front Camera (Stills)	1.2 MP	1.2 MP
Front Camera (Video)	720p HD at 30 frames/second	720p HD at 30 frames/second

Apple has never given us any definitive statement. However, I have the following opinions that I would like to share with you:

- **Most people use the rear-facing camera (almost) exclusively.** When you want to snap a picture, the natural workflow is to use the iPhone/iPad screen as a viewfinder and expose the image by using the rear-facing camera. To that end, Apple put the major camera horsepower in the camera that they felt would be used by customers most often.

- **FaceTime streaming video needs to be bandwidth-friendly.** FaceTime video chat originally worked only over Wi-Fi connections. Nowadays carriers support FaceTime, but you still need to be mindful of bandwidth as most of us pay our carrier based upon data used. Essentially, the front-facing camera is optimized for FaceTime or quick self-portraits. These self-portraits can be made more fun by editing them with the nifty Photo Booth iOS app.

iPad mini Disassembly and Reassembly

Seven-inch tablets are tweeners: too big to compete with a smartphone and too small to compete with the iPad. —Steve Jobs

The irony is delicious, I think, that when Tim Cook's Apple decided to make a smaller tablet after all, they went with a 7.9-inch diagonal screen size. Perhaps the extra 0.9 inches makes all the difference?

At any rate, I must tell you in all candor that I absolutely love my iPad mini. In point of fact, I have barely touched my full-sized iPad 3rd generation since I received my mini in the mail in late 2012.

Why do I love the iPad mini so much? Let me enumerate its major points from my personal perspective:

- The mini provides the full iPad experience in a smaller form factor.
- To the previous point, I can hold this iPad easily with one hand.
- The mini is a much more enjoyable e-reader than the full-sized iPad.
- The mini has stereo speakers.
- The mini is optimized for traveling and toting in small compartments.

Table 10.1 summarizes the iPad mini specifications.

TABLE 10.1 iPad mini Specifications

Property	Value
Release Date	November 2, 2012
OS	Apple iOS 6.0.1
Storage Capacity	16 GB, 32 GB, 64 GB
CPU	Apple A5 (same as iPad 2)
RAM	512 MB
Display Resolution	1024×768 (4:3 aspect ratio)
Pixel Density	163 pixels/in

Property	Value
Diagonal Display	7.9"
Rear Camera	5 MP with 1080p video; no flash
Front Camera	1.2 MP with 720p video
Dimensions (in.)	7.90"×5.30"×0.28"
Weight (oz)	0.68 lb for Wi-Fi model
List Price (16 GB Wi-Fi)	$329

Apple has taken quite a few steps to prevent do-it-yourselfers from attempting their own repair work on the iPad mini. On the other hand, I found the disassembly of the mini to be easier overall (at least in the initial stages) than with the full-sized iPads.

Without any further ado, let's get rocking and rolling!

External Anatomy

From an external design standpoint, the iPad mini looks like a scaled-down 4th generation iPad. Figures 10.1 through 10.4 identify the key external components of the iPad mini.

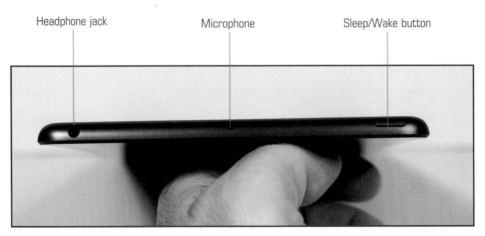

FIGURE 10.1   iPad mini top view.

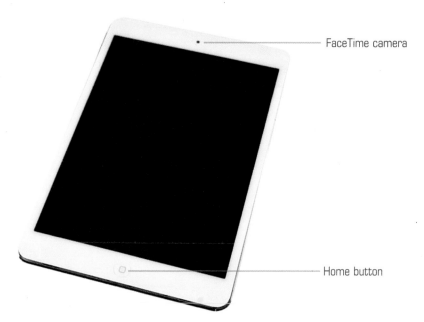

FaceTime camera

Home button

FIGURE 10.2   iPad mini front view. (Photo courtesy of ifixit.com.)

iSight camera

Side switch

Volume buttons

FIGURE 10.3   iPad mini rear view.

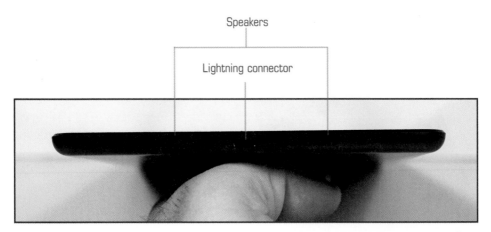

FIGURE 10.4   iPad mini bottom view.

Required Tools

- Heat gun or iFixit iOpener
- iFixit "guitar picks" (you can also use traditional, thin-gauge guitar picks if you have them handy)
- Metal and/or plastic spudger
- Plastic opening tools
- Tweezers or needle-nosed pliers
- Phillips #0 screwdriver

Disassembly Procedure

1. Use the iOpener or the heat gun to loosen the adhesive and then slide multiple "guitar picks" beneath the glass to create a wedge (see Figure 10.5). Next, run the guitar picks around the perimeter of the case until all the adhesive seals are broken.

TIP

iPad mini Screen Removal Is Tougher

As I've said in previous iPad teardowns, I cover the step-by-step behind iPad screen removal in Chapter 15, "Replacing the Front Display and/or Rear Case." However, you should know that it is easier to lift the front panel assembly on the iPad mini than it is with the full-sized iPads. I'm not exactly sure why this is the case (pun intended). There is certainly less adhesive, which goes a long way to explain the situation.

FIGURE 10.5 Prying loose the display and digitizer.

2. After you've broken through the adhesive, carefully lift the front panel assembly. As shown in Figure 10.6, do so from the top (front-facing camera) side, and lift the front panel assembly toward the bottom (Home button). Remember, the digitizer cable is still connected to the logic board.

FIGURE 10.6 Lifting up the display assembly.

3. Flip the front panel assembly over like you would open and lay flat the cover of a book.

4. Unseat the LCD. Use your Phillips #0 screwdriver to remove the four screws that are shown in Figure 10.7.

TIP

Check Under the Foam

You will find that at least two of the screws are covered (hidden might be a better term to describe it) with small wedges of foam. Carefully peel those off the screws with tweezers and be sure to replace the foam during reassembly.

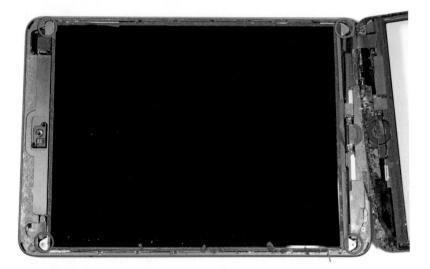

FIGURE 10.7 Remove the four screws that hold the LCD to the iPad mini rear case.

5. Use a spudger to begin to lift the LCD as shown in Figure 10.8. You need to wiggle the bottom (Home button side) of the LCD to get it to stand up straight, and then ultimately lie flat on top of the display assembly. Work slowly and carefully. You will feel some resistance as the LCD snaps through the adhesive and bends some black Kapton tape.

6. Surprise! The iPad mini includes a big ol' midplate, just like the ones that you've come to know and love in the iPod touch line. What's more, Apple ridiculously over-engineered the midplate, securing it with 16 screws (shown in Figure 10.9).

The purpose of the midplate is ostensibly to combat electromagnetic interference (EMI), but we know Apple's history of warding off us do-it-yourselfers.

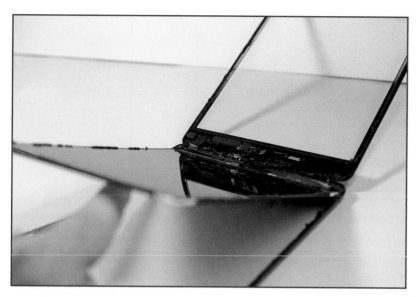

FIGURE 10.8   Lifting the LCD.

FIGURE 10.9   This midplate separates the LCD and front panel assembly from the battery and logic board.

7. Use a plastic opening tool or spudger to dislodge the midplate from the top (front-facing camera) side of the iPad mini. You might have to wiggle the midplate before it comes off completely (see Figure 10.10).

FIGURE 10.10   Removing the midplate.

8. Figure 10.11 shows the internal layout of the iPad mini. Basically you have three main areas:

   ■ Big ol' battery, the specifics of which are covered in Chapter 16, "Replacing the Battery."

   ■ Slim logic board.

   ■ Peripheral components that are attached to the logic board.

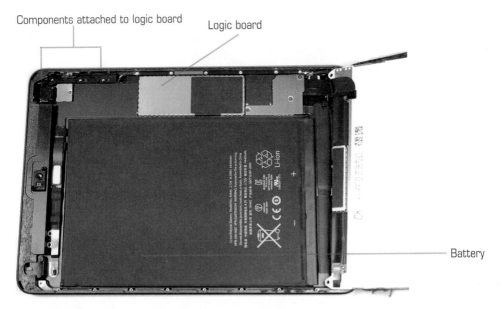

FIGURE 10.11   The interior anatomy of the iPad mini.

9. Use your trusty screwdriver to remove the three screws that hold down yet another EMI shield (see Figure 10.12). This shield covers the display cable connectors and Wi-Fi antenna connectors.

FIGURE 10.12   Removing the EMI shield that covers the display connectors.

10. Turn your attention to removing the LCD. Use your plastic opening tool or a spudger to pry the "pop" connector from its socket that leads to the LCD (see Figure 10.13).

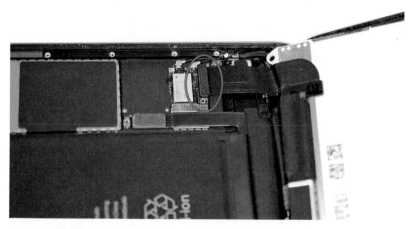

FIGURE 10.13   Disconnecting the LCD from the logic board.

CAUTION

Abundant Adhesive Ahead

Be warned: There is a copious amount of adhesive and black tape that you need to cut and/or peel back, as the case may be.

NOTE

What's That Connector?

Notice that the LCD cable connector lies on top of another connector. The second connector is how the digitizer links to the logic board (see Figure 10.14); you deal with that bad boy momentarily.

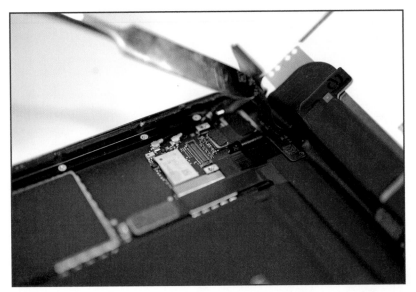

FIGURE 10.14 Lifting the LCD cable reveals the digitizer connector cable hidden underneath.

11. Carefully remove the LCD from the rest of the iPad mini and set it aside (see Figure 10.15).

TIP

Watch Out for Fingerprints

Try to handle the LCD as little as possible to limit fingerprints on the display. Keep a microfiber cloth handy to ensure a streak-free reassembly. Gloves help in this regard as well.

---

12. Use your plastic opening tool to disconnect the digitizer cable connector. However, there is more to the story. As it happens, you need to peel back the black tape behind

the digitizer cable connector. As you can see in Figure 10.16, doing so reveals a larger microcontroller that is, in turn, connected to the front panel by means of a longer ribbon cable.

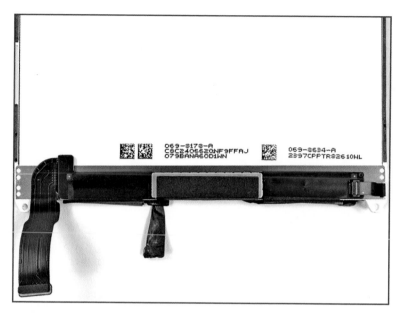

FIGURE 10.15 The disconnected LCD. That black piece in the lower middle of the LCD panel is a remnant of tape, not a separate connector.

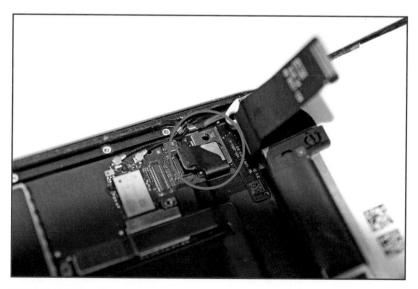

FIGURE 10.16 Exposing the digitizer microcontroller and connector. The tape has been peeled back to expose the component.

13. After you peel back the tape, you can actually use your fingers (preferably gloved) to disconnect the microcontroller and prepare the front panel for removal (see Figure 10.17). You might have to apply some heat to the area immediately surrounding the microcontroller to loosen the adhesive that holds it to the back plate. You will also doubtless need to peel more black tape and cut through additional adhesive.

FIGURE 10.17   Preparing to remove the digitizer cable from the iPad mini.

14. As you can see in Figure 10.18, the Home button assembly resides on the front panel assembly, along with the contact points. When you remove the front panel assembly, the Home button assembly is along for the ride. With other iPads, only the button itself resides on the front panel; the "guts" of the Home button's mechanical operation remain on the rear case.

15. Disconnecting the battery in the iPad mini is straightforward enough. Simply use your plastic opening tool to pry up the battery connector. The connector is shown in Figure 10.19. Note that the connector is topped with a small piece of foam; be sure to remove the connector and not the foam itself.

CAUTION

Removing the Battery Is Another Kettle of Fish

Removing the battery itself is another issue entirely. The amount of adhesive holding the battery to the rear case is significant enough that you need to use your heat gun to heat the outside of the rear case directly to give yourself any possibility of removing the battery. This is a dangerous proposition indeed, and I skipped those steps for the purposes of this chapter. That having been said, those folks who are brave enough to attempt this repair can find more than adequate tutorials online. For example, http://www.ifixit.com/Guide/Installing+ipad+mini+CDMA+Battery/12413/1 for the iPad mini is a good case in point.

FIGURE 10.18   Removing the front panel assembly from the iPad mini rear case.

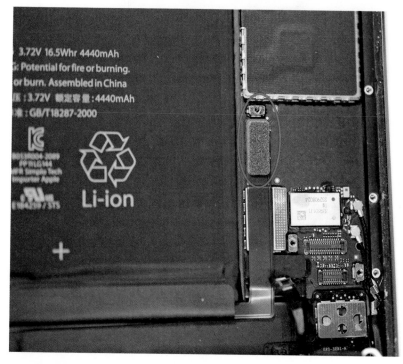

FIGURE 10.19   Disconnecting the iPad mini battery.

TIP

Logically, the Logic Board Is Glued in Place

I don't attempt to show you how to remove the logic board in this chapter. The main reason is that, believe it or not, Apple glued the logic board to the rear case. Again, the way to approach removal is to apply heat from your heat gun to the rear side of the case itself. Crazy, isn't it? I cover replacing logic boards in iDevices in Chapter 17, "Replacing the Logic Board and/or the Dock Connector."

16. The upper assembly components (headphone jack, front-facing camera, rear-facing camera, Sleep/Wake button, lock switch, and volume controls all feed into the logic board by means of a tape/adhesive-secured ribbon cable (see Figure 10.20).

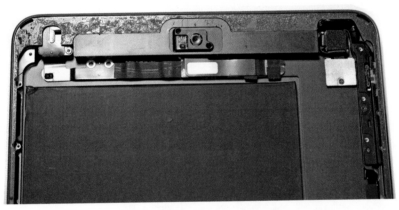

FIGURE 10.20 The upper assembly components connect to the logic board by means of a single ribbon cable.

17. At the bottom of the iPad mini is the Lightning connector and (awesome!) stereo speakers! Unfortunately, the Lightning connector is soldered directly to the logic board, as shown in Figure 10.21. This means that to replace the Lightning connector you must replace the entire logic board.

Figure 10.22 shows the requisite "blowout" shot of the fully disassembled iPad mini.

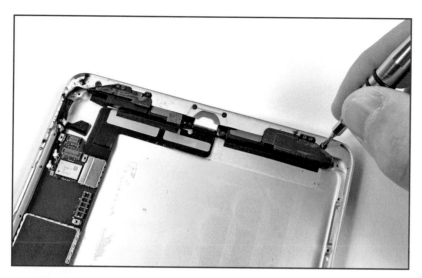

FIGURE 10.21 How the Lightning connector and speakers connect to the logic board.

FIGURE 10.22 The iPad mini, fully disassembled.

Reassembly Notes

■ You probably won't need to use adhesive strips to reseat the front panel assembly. I found that the fit and finish is such that the display popped right back into place with a minimum of force.

■ Make sure you don't snag any ribbon cables when you reseat the LCD and front panel assembly.

■ As you doubtless observed, there are many metal-to-metal contact surfaces in the mini. Therefore, consider wearing nitrile gloves and/or wiping down these surfaces during your reassembly.

■ Remember to replace the foam "covers" on the LCD screws.

What Are Benchmarks?

The following is Wikipedia's definition of *benchmark* as it relates to computing:

> *In computing, a benchmark is the act of running a computer program, a set of programs, or other operations, in order to assess the relative performance of an object, normally by running a number of standard tests and trials against it. Benchmarks provide a method of comparing the performance of various subsystems across different chip/system architectures.*

For your purposes, benchmark studies are useful because you can use their results to compare the relative performance of the following device types:

■ iDevices within a single class (for instance, comparing iPhone 4S to iPhone 5)

■ iDevices across classes (for instance, iPhone 5 to iPad 3rd generation)

■ iDevices with other platforms (for instance, comparing iOS devices to Apple's competitors)

Some benchmark tests concentrate on hardware performance exclusively. Other benchmark tests examine the performance of particular apps on different hardware.

Please note that there isn't a single (or even a group) of industry-standard benchmarking sources. Essentially anybody can run benchmark tests with iDevice hardware. What's important is that you need to standardize the tests you run as much as possible to ensure that the results are reliable.

To that end, there are benchmarking apps available to help you perform your own benchmark studies:

■ Geekbench 2 (http://is.gd/NaqEBL)

■ Gensystek Benchmark (http://is.gd/Xm8BQU)

■ iBenchmark (http://is.gd/D30wm9)

■ PaWaMark (http://is.gd/Hulcdc)

As you know, receiving data presented by websites is a matter of trust. The following list offers a number of sources for iDevice benchmark studies that are widely cited within the industry:

- Passmark Benchmarks (http://is.gd/ubvNRa)
- Geekbench (http://is.gd/D2s23I)
- GLBenchmark (http://is.gd/AQht27)
- SunSpider (http://is.gd/SB5hkk)
- Browsermark (http://is.gd/DwmYT1)

iPod touch 4th Generation Disassembly and Reassembly

Let me be perfectly blunt: I would advise you against attempting any Do-It-Yourself (DIY) disassemblies and/or repairs on any of the iPod touch models. "But this is an iPod repair guide, Tim! What are you trying to say?" I'm simply saying that Apple believes that all of its iPods (including the touches) constitute "disposable hardware." Consequently, they are manufactured with disposability and not repair in mind.

My evidence for this strong statement can be summarized by the following cogent facts that apply to all generations of the iPod touch, including the most recent model as of this writing, the iPod touch 5th generation:

- The amount of adhesive Apple uses to glue the front panel assembly to the rear case is so thick that you will have a near-impossible time getting the front panel to lie flush during reassembly.
- The front panel assembly is tethered to the bottom (!) of the logic board, and if you aren't careful you can very easily tear the cable.
- The battery and other internal components are permanently soldered (!!) to the logic board.
- The tolerance used to mount the midplane (separator panel between the front panel assembly and the battery/logic board) is so small that you will have a near-impossible time getting the piece to lie flush during reassembly.

Don't get me wrong; the iPod touch is a fine device. From a customer's point of view, I'm very happy with the 4th and 5th generation models that I own. I just want to inform you in the name of full disclosure that you are opening yourself up (pun intended) to a world of hurt if you attempt any repair on these particular iDevices.

Nevertheless, I'm including the procedure in this book for its great educational benefit. On with the show!

External Anatomy

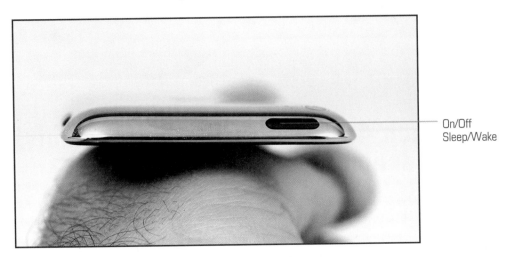

FIGURE 11.1 iPod touch 4th generation top view.

On/Off
Sleep/Wake

Volume
buttons

Front
camera

Home
button

FIGURE 11.2 iPod touch 4th generation front view.

FIGURE 11.3 iPod touch 4th generation rear view.

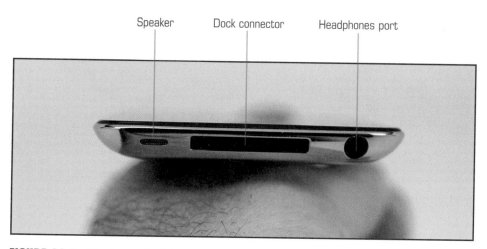

FIGURE 11.4 iPod touch 4th generation bottom view.

You can classify the iPod touch as a thinner version of the iPhone 4. However, as you'll soon see, the internal architecture of the iPod touch couldn't be more distinct from that of the iPhone.

Required Tools

- Heat gun
- Phillips #00 screwdriver
- Plastic opening tools
- Soldering iron

Disassembly Procedure

1. Using your heat gun on its lowest setting, work your way around the perimeter of the iPod touch (see Figure 11.5). Focus most of your efforts in the vicinity of the Home button.

FIGURE 11.5 Heating the front panel assembly.

2. Use a plastic opening tool to gently pry up the front panel assembly from the rear case (see Figure 11.6).

CAUTION

Look Before You Pry!

Be sure to insert the opening tool between the top two layers (front glass panel and black plastic bezel near the Home button) and not the bottom two. I've cracked a couple iPod touch screens by exerting force in the wrong area. Work slowly, carefully, and mindfully!

FIGURE 11.6 Prying up the iPod touch front panel assembly.

3. When the bottom of the front panel assembly comes loose, you can gently (stress: *gently*) lift the assembly up, as shown in Figure 11.7. Do not lift it more than 45 degrees or so up from the rear case—you will instantly observe delicate ribbon cables connecting the front panel to the logic board. Specifically, the digitizer cable

cannot be removed until you take out the logic board. Yes, I know—the construction of this device is nuts.

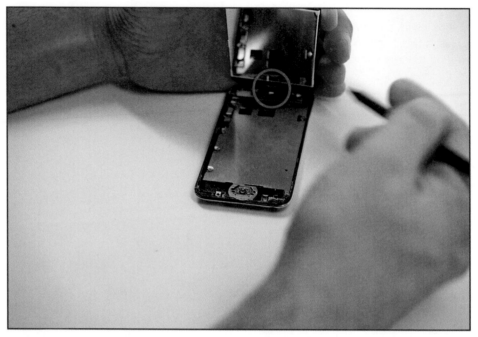

FIGURE 11.7 Lifting the front panel.

> **TIP**
>
> **Disconnect the Data Cable**
>
> To allow the display to lay flat, disconnect the display data cable. Nonetheless, be ever mindful of that display data cable!

4. You've now arrived at the annoying midplane. Remove the eight #00 Phillips screws that are marked in Figure 11.8.

5. Use the plastic opening tool to remove the delicate steel cover from the rear-facing camera (see Figure 11.9).

FIGURE 11.8   Removing the screws that hold the midplane to the rear case.

FIGURE 11.9   Removing one of many small cover pieces—this one is for the rear-facing camera.

6. Move to the lower-left corner of the midplane (near the Home button) and pry up the midplane at that corner (see Figure 11.10).

FIGURE 11.10   Beginning to pry up the midplane.

CAUTION

Watch Those Speaker Wires!

Lifting the midplane at the lower-left corner is important. However, it is even more important that you watch out for the iPod touch speaker that resides just underneath the midplane. Many a tech has severed the tiny wires by not paying enough attention during this step.

7. You should now have enough of the midplane loosened such that you can detach it from the rear case (see Figure 11.11). Again, exercise caution because the rear camera is attached to the midplane by means of a delicate piece of copper tape.

8. Use the plastic opening tool to carefully pry the headphone jack connector up from the bottom right of the rear case (see Figure 11.12).

FIGURE 11.11   Removing the midplane from the rear case.

FIGURE 11.12   Removing the headphone jack connector.

9. Remove the single Phillips #00 screw that fastens the headphone jack assembly to the iPod touch rear case (see Figure 11.13).

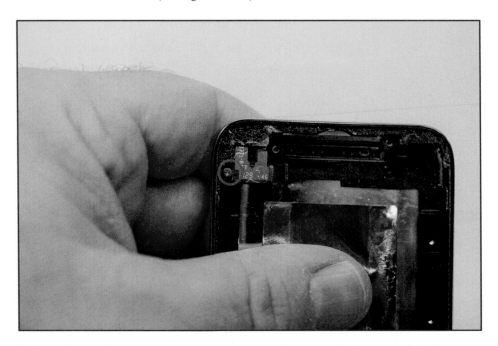

FIGURE 11.13 Removing the headphone jack assembly from the iPod touch.

10. After you remove the screw, you can use tweezers or the plastic opening tool to lift the headphone jack assembly out of the iPod touch.

11. Use the plastic opening tool to carefully pry the speaker from the rear case (see Figure 11.14).

CAUTION

Don't Break the Cable!

The speaker is tethered to the logic board by an extremely thin cable. Don't break it, or you are looking at another replacement.

12. Remove the three Phillips #00 screws at the top edge of the logic board, as shown in Figure 11.15.

FIGURE 11.14   Removing the speaker assembly (at least mostly removing it, anyway).

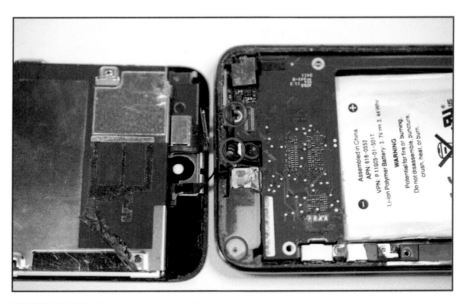

FIGURE 11.15   Removing logic board screws.

13. Use the plastic opening tool to pry the rear-facing camera out from the rear case (see Figure 11.16).

FIGURE 11.16 Removing the rear-facing camera.

14. You can now begin (stress: *begin*) the process of removing the battery from the iPod touch. Using your plastic opening tool, work your way around the frame and attempt to loosen the adhesive underneath the battery (see Figure 11.17). Please be careful not to puncture the battery cell. At this point you seek to **loosen** the battery, **not to extract it**.

15. Use the plastic opening tool to gently pry up the top of the logic board (work at the upper-right corner). After you've loosened the logic board, you can then use the plastic opening tool to push the Dock connector out of its recess. The "uprooted" Dock connector is shown in Figure 11.18.

FIGURE 11.17   Loosening the adhesive underneath the battery.

FIGURE 11.18   Freeing the Dock connector.

16. At this point you should be able to flip over the battery/logic board assembly. Don't handle the component roughly because the digitizer cable located on the underside of the logic board is still connected.

17. Use the plastic opening tool to peel off the yellow Kapton tape located near the bottom of the battery. Rotate the battery up and away from the logic board. Flip the logic board assembly over. After doing so you see the three solder joints that link the battery to the logic board (see Figure 11.19).

FIGURE 11.19 Battery/logic board solder joints.

TIP

Get Some Kapton, Captain

Kapton tape (kaptontape.com) is a polyamide film-based tape made by DuPont that is used extensively by Apple to cover and bind parts together. The cool thing about Kapton tape is that the tape remains stable (and retains its adhesion) in a range of temperatures. You might want to consider purchasing some for your personal supply.

18. It's time to call it a day at this point of this particular disassembly. Thanks to our friends at iFixit, I am happy to present you with Figure 11.20, which shows a completely disassembled iPod touch, 4th generation.

FIGURE 11.20 iPod touch 4th generation, completely disassembled. [Photo courtesy of ifixit.com.]

Reassembly Notes

There are no two ways about it: You need to find an adhesive solution for holding the iPod touch components together during reassembly. In my experience, your best bet is to invest in plenty of the following products:

- **3M 3703 Tape:** You can use this electrically conductive tape to secure the Wi-Fi ribbon cables to the logic board. Find it online at the 3M site at http://is.gd/GF71mF.

- **3M Adhesive Sticker Tape:** You can find sellers who vend this tape pre-cut to match the dimensions of your iPod touch model. For instance, try finding it at TVC-Mall at http://is.gd/ZC0Ocf.

- **3M 300LSE Low Surface Energy Acrylic Adhesive Transfer Tape:** (Try to say that five times quickly!) 3M 300LSE Low Surface Energy Acrylic Adhesive Transfer Tape is the specific type of tape used in the precut stickers. You can read about it at the 3M site: http://is.gd/YCw6LB.

Is the iPod touch a "Watered Down" iPhone?

Steve Jobs once famously described the iPod touch as "training wheels" for the iPhone. Some customers believe that they can derive every benefit of the iPhone (with the exception of cellular service) by purchasing an iPod touch. Frankly, the price point between the touches and the iPhones has always been surprisingly close.

However, much has been written on comparing the hardware specifications between the iPod touch and the iPhone, and the results point definitively that the iPod touch is in many ways a solidly inferior device, performance-wise, to its corresponding iPhone model.

Take the so-called Retina display, for example. Apple's marketing literature brags that the iPod touch 4th generation and the iPhone 4 both share the following display features:

- 3.5-inch (diagonal) widescreen multi-touch display.
- 960×640 pixel resolution at 326 pixels/inch. (Four times the number of pixels as pre-Retina displays at the same resolution; the idea is that the eye cannot discern individual pixels when viewing a Retina display.)

However, it is now common knowledge that the iPod touch does not use the in-plane switching (IPS) LCD display technology that is implemented on the iPhone 4S. Rather, the iPod touch uses the more common twisted nematic (TN) LCD display technology. I'll tell you, friends: I have worked with the iPhone 4S and the 4th generation iPod touch side-by-side, and there is a noticeable difference in clarity between the two displays. So much so, in point of fact, that I wondered if the touch's display actually could be called "Retina" outside of its presence in Apple's marketing materials.

NOTE

The Skinny on IPS

IPS technology is also used by Apple with its LED Cinema displays and in the iPads. The main selling points about IPS are that that they offer superior color reproduction and they convey a wider viewing angle than that of a typical, non-IPS LCD (like the iPod touch 4th generation).

The rear camera is another sore spot of contention between the two analogous devices. For one thing, the iPod touch rear-facing camera lacks the flash that is present on the iPhone 4S. Also, the iPod touch rear-facing camera shoots at 0.7 megapixels (MP), whereas the iPhone 4S shoots at 8 MP. Those are some significant differences, in my opinion.

When you compare the list prices of the two devices, it seems to me that you take a substantial feature hit by selecting the iPod touch.

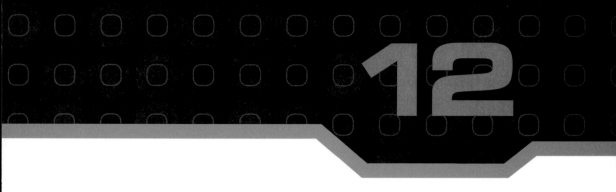

iPod nano 5th and 7th Generation Disassembly and Reassembly

I definitely have a soft spot in my heart for the iPod nano. Sure, I can play music on my iPod touches or my iPhones. However, you just can't beat the portability of the nano. I also enjoy that the nano has always been a single-purpose device.

When I'm out running with my nano in my pocket, I am not tempted to check my email or jump online because those options simply are not available to me. The nano is a simple device and is relatively easy to take apart if you are willing to accept the following statement as truth:

After you disassemble an iPod nano, there is little to no chance that you can reassemble it to the way it was before you tore it apart.

The previous remark speaks to the "disposability" aspect of the nano. I can essentially guarantee you that although you may be able to disassemble and reassemble the nano successfully, the fit and finish might be off, there might be cosmetic damage, or both.

NOTE

Use the Right Nomenclature

Please remember how important it is to use our terminology precisely. Avoid calling the 5th generation iPod nano "iPod nano 5G." Remember that we use the G designation to denote carrier network speed. Moreover, Apple stylizes this product name as "iPod nano," not "iPod Nano." I don't mean to get distracted by semantics here, friends—I simply want to ensure that we understand each other when we talk shop.

In this chapter I selected the 5th generation nano for the primary teardown subject. My reasons for doing this are as follows:

- Nowadays, all iDevices use capacitive touch screens. Including an iDevice with the old-school tactile scroll wheel adds a sense of history and nostalgia to this book.

- The 5th (and 4th) generation nanos have a very interesting method of construction; it's the ultimate in space-saving efficiency.

- The 5th generation iPod nano is my favorite model of all nano models.

In Table 12.1, you can see that the 5th gen nano holds its own quite nicely as compared to the latest (as of this writing) 7th generation model.

TABLE 12.1 Comparison Between iPod nano 5th Generation and iPod nano 7th Generation

Property	5th gen nano	7th gen nano
Date of introduction	September 13, 2009	October 12, 2012
Capacities	8GB or 16GB	16GB
Dimensions	3.6"×1.5"×.24"	3.01"×1.56"×.21"
Weight	1.28oz.	1.10oz.
Display	240×376 pixel resolution at 204 pixels/inch	240×432 pixel resolution at 202 pixel/inch
Camera	.3 MP (video only)	none
Case	Polished aluminum	Anodized aluminum

External Anatomy

Figures 12.1 through 12.4 show you the external structure of the iPod nano 5th generation.

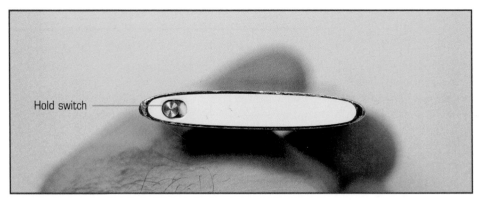

Hold switch

FIGURE 12.1 iPod nano 5th generation top view.

Center button   Click wheel   Microphone   Lens

FIGURE 12.2   iPod nano 5th
generation front view.

FIGURE 12.3   iPod nano 5th
generation rear view.

Headphone port   30-pin connector

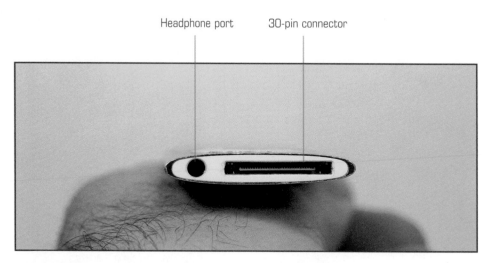

FIGURE 12.4 iPod nano 5th generation bottom view.

Just for grins, compare Figures 12.1 through 12.4 with Figures 12.5 through 12.8, which shows the external organization of the iPod nano 7th generation, the latest version as of this writing in spring 2013.

Sleep/Wake button

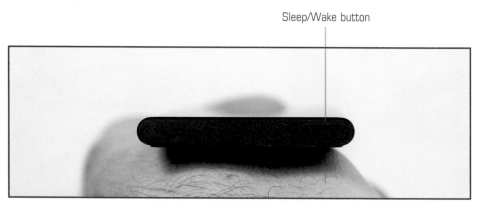

FIGURE 12.5 iPod nano 7th generation top view.

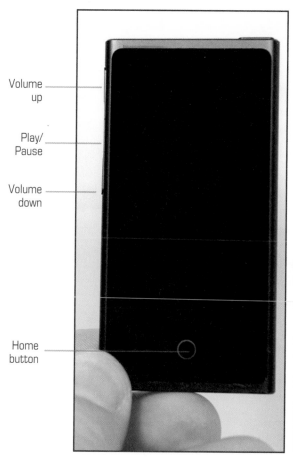

Volume up

Play/ Pause

Volume down

Home button

FIGURE 12.6 iPod nano 7th generation front view.

FIGURE 12.7 iPod nano 7th generation rear view.

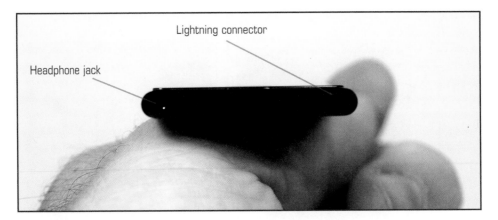

FIGURE 12.8 iPod nano 7th generation bottom view.

On with the show! Let's start by performing a full teardown of the 5th generation nano. I follow that up with a mini-teardown of the 7th generation nano.

Required Tools

- Heat gun
- Phillips #00 screwdriver
- Metal spudger and plastic opening tools
- Tweezers
- iFixit "guitar picks" (you can use traditional, thin-gauge guitar picks if you have them)
- Soldering iron

Disassembly Procedure

1. Start at the top of the nano. Use a metal or plastic opening tool to gently pry the top bezel off the iPod nano (see Figure 12.9). As expected, you encounter quite a bit of resistance from the liberal amount of adhesive used to bind the components together.

2. Use your plastic opening tool to pry the hold switch button off the hold switch plate. This component comes off the nano completely.

3. While you're at it, use your screwdriver to remove the two retaining screws that I call out in Figure 12.10.

FIGURE 12.9   Removing the top panel.

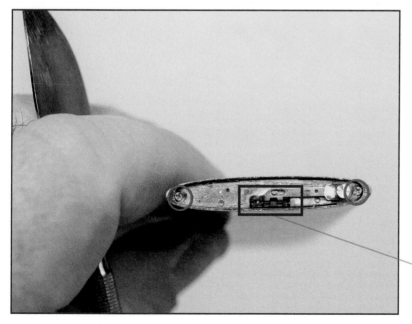

The pause
switch
connects to
the logic board
here

FIGURE 12.10   Removing the hold switch button and retaining screws.

TIP

Screws Inserted at Angle

These screws are angled in from the edge of the iPod. Be mindful not to strip the screw heads during your work.

4. Use your plastic opening tool to pull the hold switch plate out of the nano (see Figure 12.11).

CAUTION

Slow Down!

I can't stress this enough: Work slowly because the hold switch plate is tethered to the iPod nano by means of a delicate ribbon cable. It is far too easy to rip this ribbon cable.

FIGURE 12.11 Removing the hold switch plate.

5. Lift out the glass screen by inserting your plastic opening tool between the outer case and the top-left or right edge of the glass panel as shown in Figure 12.12. A common technique is to lift the display a bit, slide a guitar pick or another opening tool into the gap to hold it open, and then apply pressure in another location on the panel. Your goal is to loosen the liberal adhesive that holds the glass in place.

FIGURE 12.12   Removing the glass panel.

6. Turn your attention to the bottom of the nano. Use a heat gun, on the lowest setting, to loosen the adhesive that holds the bottom bezel on the nano. Remove the bezel by using your plastic opening tool. Figure 12.13 shows the loosened bezel being removed.

7. Use your Phillips #00 screwdriver to remove the three retaining screws on the bottom of the nano (see Figure 12.14). Again, the two outer screws are angled inward and are therefore extremely easy to strip.

8. When the screws are gone, take out the retaining clip for the 30-pin connector.

FIGURE 12.13 Removing the bottom bezel.

FIGURE 12.14 Removing the retaining screws on the iPod nano.

9. Remove the click wheel by inserting a metal spudger into the slot above the Dock connector and gently prying up the bottom edge of the click wheel (see Figure 12.15). You can insert the spudger or an iFixit guitar pick into the gap underneath the click

wheel. You can then slowly work your way around the click wheel until it pops out of the nano completely.

FIGURE 12.15   Removing the click wheel using a pair of spudgers.

10. To remove the click wheel entirely, lift the click wheel out of the way with one hand and use a plastic opening tool to pry the click wheel ribbon cable connector from the logic board (see Figure 12.16). Note that the figure does not show the plastic opening tool.

FIGURE 12.16 After lifting the click wheel, use a plastic opening tool to pry the click wheel ribbon from the logic board.

11. You might need to use your heat gun to soften the adhesive underneath the camera/microphone cover located on the back of the nano. Next, use a metal spudger to pry up the camera/microphone cover, as shown in Figure 12.17. Be prepared: You will likely scratch the paint on your nano in performing this step.

FIGURE 12.17 Removing the camera/microphone cover.

12. There is a small white retainer between the camera and microphone that keeps the inner components from sliding around. Insert a pushpin into the hole at the corner of the retainer and lift it out of the case.

13. Insert your metal spudger between the outer case and the battery and try to dislodge as much adhesive as possible (see Figure 12.18). Your goal is to slide the battery and logic board assembly out of the outer case like you'd remove a stick of chewing gum from its package.

FIGURE 12.18   Loosening the battery adhesive.

14. Now comes the fun part. Using a plastic spudger, push the logic board assembly through the outer case and out the bottom (see Figure 12.19). Be patient, and remember that the hold switch assembly is still tethered to the logic board by means of that crazily thin ribbon cable.

15. You should be able to lift the battery perpendicular to the logic board. At the same time, observe a number of solder pads holding the battery to the logic board. Use tweezers to remove the strip of yellow tape that covers those pads (see Figure 12.20).

FIGURE 12.19 Extracting the logic board, LCD, and battery from the outer case.

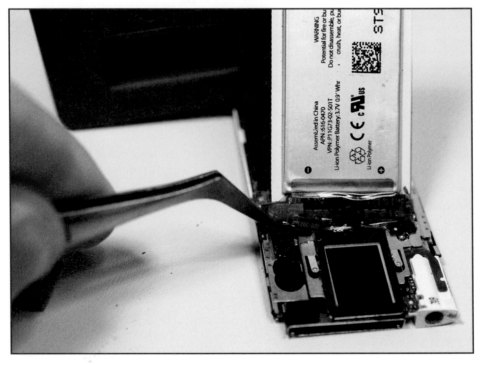

FIGURE 12.20 Uncovering the battery solder pads.

16. If you need to replace the battery and are brave, you can use your solder gun to desolder the battery from the logic board; I've highlighted the solder pads in Figure 12.21.

FIGURE 12.21   The battery solder joints revealed.

Thanks to our friends at iFixit, Figure 12.22 shows a completely disassembled iPod nano 5th generation; you should recognize all of the parts in the following image.

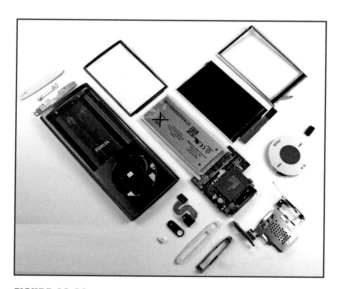

FIGURE 12.22   The iPod nano 5th generation, completely disassembled. (Photo courtesy of ifixit.com.)

NOTE

iPod nano 7th Gen Disassembly

If you want a complete walkthrough of iPod nano 7th Gen disassembly, see the wiki page at iFixit (http://is.gd/rRlxv1).

iPod nano 5th Generation Reassembly Notes

- If you happen to sever the hold switch ribbon cable, don't worry about it too much. The iPod will still work, although you obviously won't be able to lock it. (That is a deal breaker for me, however, because I love the mechanical controls on this generation of the nano.)

- You will doubtless need to "rob Peter to pay Paul" inasmuch as getting the nano back together requires you to co-op and re-use as much adhesive as you can from the disassembly. The good news is that the logic board, battery, and LCD slide into the main case. The bad news is that your iPod nano will likely not retain its original fit and finish.

iPod nano 7th Generation Quick-Disassembly

In this section we provide a (very) high-level schematic overview of iPod nano 7th generation disassembly.

The good news is that you can use the same tools you used for the 5th generation disassembly.

1. Use your plastic opening tool to remove the tab at the lower back of the nano, as shown in Figure 12.23. This little tab is the "magic door" through which the rest of the disassembly is accomplished.

2. Pry up the display assembly from the rear case by applying your plastic opening tool to the seam at the side of the case. (See Figure 12.24 for an example of how it looks after it's been opened.)

CAUTION

Wires Abound

Expect plenty of adhesive and hidden wires. This iDevice was NOT intended for do-it-yourself repair, I promise you.

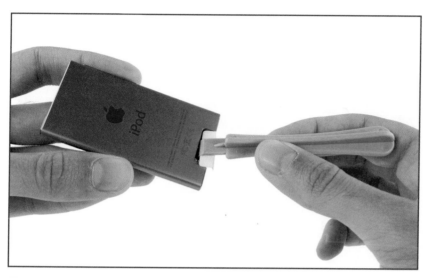

FIGURE 12.23   Beginning the nano 7th generation disassembly. (Photo courtesy of ifixit.com.)

FIGURE 12.24   Cracking open the 7th generation nano. (Photo courtesy of ifixit.com.)

3. Figure 12.25 shows the exploded, fully disassembled nano. To me the most interesting component is the new Lightning connector, which replaces the old 30-pin Dock connector we've grown to love (or at least grudgingly tolerate) over the years. I spend a lot of time talking about the Lightning connector later on in this book.

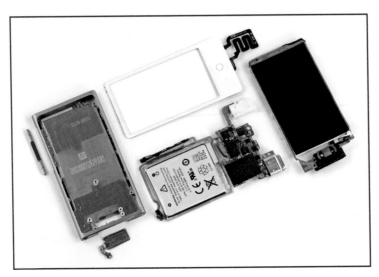

FIGURE 12.25   The 7th generation nano, fully disassembled. (Photo courtesy of ifixit.com.)

About the Mysterious Pixo OS

As you know, the 6th and 7th generation iPod nanos have touch screen interfaces and support limited finger gestures. The nano 7th gen interface in particular looks particularly iOS-like. But does the nano actually run a stripped-down version of the iOS?

Apple certainly isn't telling us anything, but the industry consensus says "no." Consider the following facts, some of which I sourced from an excellent blog post from Roughlydrafted. com (http://is.gd/QZcG13):

- The Home button on the 7th generation iPod nano uses a circle icon to differentiate the device from the iPhone/iPod touch/iPad Home buttons, which feature a square-shaped icon.
- The apps included on the iPod nano are round, whereas app icons in iOS are square.
- The current iPod nano has absolutely no internet connectivity or capability of running iOS apps.
- The prevailing belief is that the iPod nano runs what is called the Pixo OS. Pixo has been around since 1994, and at one time, early in the iPod nano's lifecycle, Apple credited Pixo OS in its About iPod menu. Additional evidence that points toward Pixo OS driving the nanos lies in the fact that Pixo was founded by former Apple employees; specifically members of the Newton project.

Sourcing iDevice Replacement Parts

This part of the book covers how to perform a series of parts replacements. I selected the specific replacements based upon my extensive experience in supporting Apple desktop and mobile hardware.

Because the subsequent chapters assume that you have the relevant replacement parts on hand, you might have the following question:

- Where can I find iDevice parts?
- How can I ensure that I get Original Equipment Manufacturer (OEM) parts and not cheap imitations?

I decided this topic needs a separate chapter because I have some big-time *caveat emptor* (buyer beware) tips and tricks for you in locating replacement parts. Let's get started.

What Is OEM, and Why Do I Care?

The acronym OEM denotes Original Equipment Manufacturer, and I'm sad to inform you that the term is used in the industry in confusing and sometimes contradictory ways.

Wikipedia formally defines OEM this way:

> *An original equipment manufacturer, or OEM, manufactures products or components that are purchased by another company and retailed under that purchasing company's brand name. OEM refers to the company that originally manufactured the product.*

Are you with me so far? Pay particular attention to that last sentence. The Wikipedia article goes on to say:

> *OEM may refer to a company that purchases for use in its own products a component made by a second company. Under this definition, if Apple purchases optical drives from Toshiba to put in its computers, Apple is the OEM, and Toshiba would classify the transaction as an "OEM sale."*

If you examine most Apple hardware, you'll find statements such as the one shown in Figure 13.1.

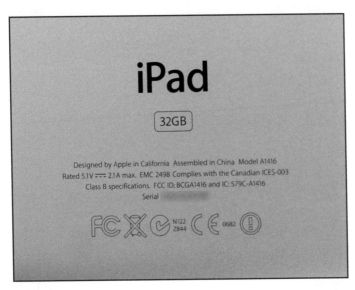

FIGURE 13.1 Apple's OEM disclaimer on the back panel of an iPad 3rd generation.

The Taiwan-based Foxconn Technology Group (www.foxconn.com) has been in the news quite a bit over the past several years. Leaving the controversial stuff aside, the public knows that Foxconn is one of Apple's OEM partners. Foxconn manufactures iDevice components, and they are stamped with Apple's brand name. Thus, all of these parts are Apple OEM parts.

The trick is how can we, the everyday, standalone iDevice techs, get our mitts on OEM replacement parts for iDevices? Officially, only Apple Authorized Service Providers (AASPs) have the ability to order OEM replacement parts through the online Apple Global Service Exchange (https://gsx.apple.com) website.

Thus, our "unofficial" method for sourcing OEM iDevice replacement parts means turning to the wild and wooly world of the Internet.

Some might argue, "What's the big deal about OEM parts? If I can buy a touch screen/ LCD/digitizer replacement for a good price and it works, then why do I care if the part is OEM or not?"

The sad truth is that you will find, in general, a quality difference between Apple OEM and aftermarket parts. Consider the touchscreen. Apple uses Corning Gorilla Glass (corninggorillaglass.com) to provide a perfect blend of clarity, thinness, lightness, and damage resistance to all its iDevices.

However, you would be hard-pressed ever to find Gorilla Glass used in an aftermarket, non-OEM display assembly. Why? Two reasons: (a) production cost; and (b) Corning has an exclusive agreement with Apple to provide Gorilla Glass for its iDevices.

Where Can I Find OEM iDevice Parts?

Before I give you a punch list of iDevice parts sources that I recommend to you, I want to lead off by providing you with a couple tidbits of advice that you can take action on immediately.

No Guarantees

Unless you buy the part directly from Apple, there is no guarantee that the part you receive is genuine OEM.

If you search the Internet, you will discover web content (typically from parts resellers) that offers tips for determining whether a given iDevice replacement part is genuine OEM or an aftermarket copy.

Please don't believe any of that nonsense. The only 100 percent sure method for receiving Apple OEM parts is to order them directly from Apple. OEM partners such as Foxconn aren't allowed to sell parts directly to consumers. Again, you must be an AASP in order to gain access to the parts requisition process.

What's especially heinous is that there are companies out there who copy iDevice parts (even entire iDevices, for that matter) and go so far as to reproduce Apple-specific markings.

For instance, take a look at the close-up of an iPod touch 4th gen's internals in Figure 13.2. How can you tell whether the markings you see on the LCD and digitizer represent OEM or a third-party knock-off?

FIGURE 13.2 Apple OEM components are typically marked, but this doesn't guarantee that a similarly marked replacement part is OEM.

Study Buyer Reviews

Study buyer reviews carefully, and make personal contacts if possible.

As you know, online marketplaces such as Amazon.com and eBay.com have rich community support. Make sure that you thoroughly read buyer reviews before you place an order with an iDevice repair parts provider.

What's even more effective is if you can obtain a personal referral from a colleague, friend, or fellow online buyer. Don't be afraid to directly contact buyers who leave worthwhile reviews on shopping sites. Online purchases are often a complete "shot in the dark" unless you have verified experience of other buyers to rely upon beforehand.

Trust Your Gut

When working with an aftermarket vendor, go with your intuition.

When you do "take the plunge" and place an order with an aftermarket iDevice parts vendor, pay attention to the entire process. Take the time to consider the following questions:

- Based upon your interactions, is the vendor worthy of trust?
- Would you recommend this vendor to others?
- How communicative is the vendor? Does he keep you informed of order status?
- How willing is the vendor to handle returns or refunds?

But Where Do I Start My Search?

Given these admittedly depressing warnings, what websites would I recommend to you in your search of OEM iDevice parts? Here you go:

- **Amazon** (http://amazon.com): Read the buyer reviews carefully.
- **eBay** (http://ebay.com): Same advice concerning reading buyer reviews.
- **iFixit** (http://www.ifixit.com/iPhone-Parts): I'm not 100 percent sure that their parts are OEM. However, they offer a warranty and installation instructions—can't beat that!
- **AppleOEMParts** (http://www.appleoemparts.com): This company offers free shipping for most parts.
- **eTechParts** (http://www.etechparts.com/): This company boasts impressive customer support.

A word of warning: Be sure to read the return/warranty policy for online iDevice parts vendors. Sometimes a vendor does not offer return or replacement policies, which might leave you with Dead on Arrival (DOA) parts. On the other hand, iFixit offers wholesale parts and tool discounts with established return and warranty policies

Grim Realities

I apologize for being the bearer of bad news, but I hope you know me well enough by now to trust that I'm going to tell you the straight story without any Apple-correct filtering.

I have had a significant number of iDevice replacement parts fail. Either the part didn't work out of the box, or its cheap construction resulted in breakage shortly after the repair (see Figure 13.3). This sad truth underscores the following two points:

- When you find a vendor who ships you quality parts, stick with that vendor!
- Consider purchasing more than one instance of each replacement part.

FIGURE 13.3   Would you be surprised if I told you the "OEM" replacement display I ordered for my iPhone 4S (shown installed at left) doesn't work? Don't be—it was dead on arrival (DOA).

If your plan is to work part-time or full-time as an iDevice tech then you should have a robust supply of replacement parts on hand anyway. Please take the necessary steps to ensure that you aren't reliant upon a single replacement part to save the day.

Addressing Water Damage

Whenever I run, I take either my iPhone or one of my iPods with me so that I can enjoy listening to an audiobook while I exercise. Because I live in the sunny southeastern United States, the weather is typically dry, so I have no worries.

However, what about a wet, rainy day? If a few stray raindrops fall upon my iDevice, could this cause damage? What if you drop your iDevice in a puddle of rainwater? Or the kitchen sink? What if you spill a can of soda directly on top of your iPad?

The ways in which water or other liquids can enter your iDevice case are innumerable. The goal of this chapter is to describe exactly what damage water can cause an iDevice and then present invasive and non-invasive methods for addressing a waterlogged Apple mobile device.

I want to make sure you are armed with the facts concerning water damage to electronics, effective methods for addressing the problem when it occurs, and (perhaps most importantly) steps you can take to limit the possibility of water damage occurring in the first place.

The Problem of Water Damage

Water poses a very real threat to all electronic devices, not only iDevices. The danger lies in the fact that water conducts electricity. Thus, when water contacts the integrated circuits inside your iDevice, water helpfully attempts to continue any current that may be flowing.

If the iDevice is powered on at the time it gets wet (which is usually the case, sadly), the extra current flow produced by the water can cause a variety of immediate problems:

- Electrical shorts and overloads, which burn out components
- Erratic re-routing of electrical current, causing unpredictable iDevice behavior
- Damage to the battery, which can present a chemical and/or fire hazard
- Corrosion

The fourth bullet point in the previous list bears further explanation. If you don't address a liquid incursion immediately then you create fertile ground for corrosion (rust) to take place within your iDevice. This corrosion impedes the flow of electricity and renders some or all of your iDevice inoperable.

This chapter focuses specifically on water, but the introduction of other liquids, such as soda, causes additional problems. The issue here is that these beverages contain chemicals and properties beyond simple water— think of sugar, salt, and carbonation.

When non-water liquids dry on the surface of your iDevice's integrated circuits, they leave behind their sugary/salty residue. Impeded current flow means a "bricked" iDevice.

Okay. I think I've made my point that you want to do everything possible to limit the introduction of water into any of your iDevices. Next, it's time to address the following question: Does AppleCare cover water damage?

Warranty Ramifications of Water Damage

Do either the Apple Hardware Warranty or AppleCare cover water damage? Yes, but only if you bought AppleCare+.

There is no provision for water damage coverage in either the Apple Hardware Warranty or the traditional AppleCare Protection Plan. However, if you are fortunate enough to have AppleCare+ coverage for your iDevice then, yes, you can receive a replacement device (subject to the service fee, naturally). Here is the relevant line from the AppleCare+ Terms and Conditions document for the iPhone (http://is.gd/0CppGy). I added the bold for emphasis:

> *Accidental Damage and Handling (ADH) coverage only applies to an operational or mechanical failure caused by an accident from handling that is the result of an unexpected and unintentional external event (e.g., drops and liquid contact) that arises from your normal daily usage of the Covered iPhone as intended for such Covered iPhone.*

Liquid Contact Indicators (LCIs) and You

All iPhones, iPads, and iPod touches built after 2006 contain several Liquid Contact Indicators (LCIs) that alert Apple Store personnel if the iDevice has experienced liquid contact.

The LCIs are white paper dots that turn red in the presence of liquid. See Figure 14.1 for an example.

Generally speaking, you can look for LCIs in the following locations on an iDevice:

- Inside the headphone jack (shine a flashlight directly down the jack)
- Within the Dock connector
- Above the logic board on an electromagnetic interference (EMI) shield

An Apple Store Genius can quickly assess an iDevice for water damage by checking two exterior LCIs and then popping off the rear case and examining the interior LCIs.

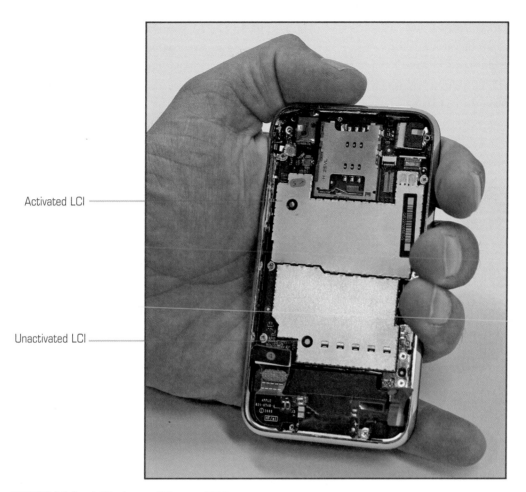

Activated LCI

Unactivated LCI

FIGURE 14.1   LCIs in an iPhone 3GS.

Much has been written online about how to "game" Apple Store personnel by attempting to replace or reset the LCIs. I suggest you avoid these parlor tricks.

The following non-invasive methods for addressing water damage are great for non-technicians (which is to say, the majority of Apple's customer base). However, you and I are iDevice techs, so we can leverage more invasive and effective methods for drying these devices. I cover those later in this chapter.

How to Address a Waterlogged iDevice: Non-Invasive Approach

Regardless of which of the following two methods I provide you with for addressing a waterlogged iDevice, the first rule is the same for both:

Power off your iDevice completely. Do not put it to sleep—*power it off.*

Given our previous discussion on the hows and whys of water damage, I trust you understand why you need to remove power from your device without any delay.

You also should rotate and shake the powered-off iDevice to let any pent-up water drain from the chassis.

The Rice Method

After your device is powered off, what then? If you don't have any dedicated tools for resolving water-damaged electronics (more on that in just a minute) then perform the following procedure:

1. Fill a bowl with uncooked rice. No, I'm not kidding. Be sure that the container has an airtight lid.

2. Dry off the exterior of your iDevice as much as you can with a towel.

3. If applicable, remove the SIM tray and SIM card.

4. Submerge your iDevice into the rice and seal the container.

5. Leave the iDevice covered up in the rice for two or three days. Periodically change the orientation of the iDevice within the rice in order to let gravity and the rice work together to draw all moisture out of the iDevice.

6. Retrieve the iDevice from the rice, remove all rice remnants from the device, power it on, and test functionality.

Dedicated Drying Tools

If you want to proactively address the possibility of iDevice water damage then you should consider purchasing a quantity of silica gel packets. You can purchase these from Amazon.com or several other online sources. As you probably know, silica gel is great at quickly removing moisture from whatever moisture containing objects it contacts.

In case you were wondering, silica gel is a far more effective desiccant (drying agent) than uncooked rice.

Another possibility is the Thirsty Bag, sold by (guess who?) iFixit. You can see one in Figure 14.2.

Essentially, the Thirsty Bag is a paper bag that is filled with silica gel packets. Here's how you use it:

1. Put the powered off, toweled-off iDevice into the Thirsty Bag. Seal the bag.

2. Wait 24 hours.

3. Remove and test the iDevice.

FIGURE 14.2   iFixit Thirsty Bag. (Photo courtesy of ifixit.com.)

How to Address a Waterlogged iDevice: Invasive Approach

After powering off, toweling off, and shaking your waterlogged iDevice, follow these steps:

1. Open the case and disconnect the battery. This is crucial because the battery is the DC power source for the iDevice when it isn't plugged into an AC socket or a USB port. Consult the proper disassembly chapter in this book to help you safely open your iDevice.

2. Disassemble the iDevice and carefully dry exposed components with a microfiber or other lint-free cloth.

3. To be sure that you've cleaned the internal components, you should obtain isopropyl alcohol in at least 90 percent concentration (check online or in your local pharmacy) and submerge the logic board and other affected parts.

CAUTION

Isopropyl Alcohol Only!

Be absolutely sure to use isopropyl alcohol. Using any other form of alcohol risks causes irreparable damage to your iDevice components.

4. Use a toothbrush or small paintbrush to scrub the logic board; this assists in the loosening and removal of built-up debris (especially helpful for coffee and soft drink liquid incursion). Also, pay special attention to connectors and contacts. Be gentle when you brush these delicate components.

5. After removing the logic board and any other components from their isopropyl alcohol bath, use a hair dryer on its coolest setting to dry the components. The good news is that isopropyl alcohol evaporates extremely quickly at room temperature.

6. If you have a spare battery in your workspace stockpile, it's advisable to replace the battery.

7. Reassemble your device and run tests to verify that the device works properly. You still run the high risk of having to replace the LCD and/or the logic board, but you have certainly mitigated against further, longer-term damage to the device.

How to Limit the Possibility of Water Damage

In the name of proactivity, I want to conclude this chapter by suggesting how you can limit the possibility of water damage to your iDevices.

Purchase a Specialty Case

The best defense against water damage for your iDevice is to invest in a specialty case. Read the box and marketing copy for these products carefully—many iDevice covers offer water resistance, but not waterproofing. Also, pay attention to the reviews of customers to help you make the best choice.

Here are a few products that are highly rated and offer water protection for your iDevice:

- Lifeproof (http://www.lifeproof.com)
- Liquipel (http://www.liquipel.com/)
- Dry Case (http://www.drycase.com/)

Limit Exposure to Steam

Some people use iDevices in the bathroom when we shower. For instance, I like to listen to audiobooks by connecting my iPhone or iPod to an external power amp and speaker set. The hazard here is condensation. A steamy bathroom can result in water condensation inside your iDevice. Not only can the condensed water louse up the device's mechanics, but it can also trip the LCIs.

Use a Low-Tech Plastic Baggie

Runners like me need to come up with inventive ways to protect our iDevices against potential water damage. Try wrapping your iDevice in a zipper-top plastic baggie. Squeeze out as much extra air as you can, and close the zipper against the headphone cord.

If you have some silica gel packets, you could add one or two packets to the iDevice/baggie combination for an extra measure of protection.

15

Replacing the Front Display and/or Rear Case

By far the most common iDevice repair issue is a broken front display or rear case. Let's face it—we humans are prone to dropping our iDevices. Moreover, a majority of iDevice users tend to be more concerned with fashionable or cool-looking iDevice cases rather than a case that actually protects against a drop.

Let's see if I can give you a couple examples from my personal experiences. There was the time when my iPod touch came out of my pocket during a run and landed facedown on a rock—ouch. My super-deluxe armored case didn't prevent the front display from looking like a spider built a web across it.

Then there was the time when my two-year-old daughter, Zoey, wanted to "play" with my iPhone 4S. I think you can take that scenario to its logical conclusion without further prompting. As I've told you before, as you start your work as an iDevice repair technician, you can rest assured that you'll break some glass along the way, especially when you try to separate the front glass from iPads.

For proof of this, take a look at Figure 15.1, which shows you an iPad 2 display assembly that shattered spectacularly during a repair.

FIGURE 15.1 iPad 2 display assembly—or what's left of it—after a failed attempt at front glass removal.

With respect to front and rear glass replacements, I have some good news and some bad news. The good news is that a couple iDevice models make the process relatively trouble-free. The bad news is that other iDevices models make the process extraordinarily difficult.

I begin the discussion with a description of how the display assembly of an iDevice actually works. If you've followed the iDevice disassemblies in the preceding chapters of this book then you already have a pretty good idea as to what's what.

Anatomy of the iDevice Front Display

In Figure 15.2, I attempt to present a logical depiction of a typical iDevice's front display assembly. The word "assembly" is key because the front display isn't a single component; it's a combination of three separate parts.

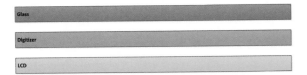

FIGURE 15.2   Schematic illustration of the iDevice front display assembly.

The glass itself is made of Corning Gorilla Glass (http://www.corninggorillaglass.com). Gorilla Glass is an alkali-aluminosilicate sheet glass that is renowned for its lightness, thinness, and damage resistance.

> **NOTE**
>
> **Heart of (Gorilla) Glass**
>
> Although we can reasonably assume that Apple uses Gorilla Glass on all contemporary iDevices, the iPhone is the only device to which Apple has openly admitted applying the technology (Reference: http://is.gd/2EV3Wa).

The digitizer is the electronic component that senses the touch of the human finger (or capacitive stylus) and translates those location coordinates to a digital stream that is passed to the iDevice logic board. Because the digitizer, which looks like a transparent sheet, is wholly reliant upon the front glass for its operation, you'll find that the glass and digitizer are always fused together.

This glass/digitizer combination constitutes the *capacitive touch screen* that so many people rave about with iDevices and some other smart devices. In brief, capacitive touch screens use the human finger or a capacitive stylus as an electrical conductor; the touch creates a distortion of the screen's electrostatic field that is measured, quantified, and as I said earlier, transferred to the logic board as user input.

Finally, the Liquid Crystal Display (LCD) is the actual viewable screen of an iDevice that represents graphical output (and provides a target for input) for the iDevice user.

The rear case of an iDevice isn't terribly interesting, quite honestly. Either the rear case is made of breakable glass, or it is made of plastic or aluminum.

From a repair perspective, it is important that you discover how Apple kits each iDevice with respect to its front display assembly and rear case components. To that end, I've assembled this data for most of the contemporary iDevice models in Table 15.1.

NOTE

You Say Tomato

There seems to be no real consistency in nomenclature when referring to the iDevice rear case. You'll see various references to *rear case, back plate, backplate, rear cover*, and more. As long as you know and I both know what part we're talking about, we're good to go.

In the Front Display Setup table column, *fused* means that the glass, digitizer, and LCD are fused into a single part.

TABLE 15.1 iDevice Display Comparison Matrix

Device	Front Display Setup	Rear Case Composition
iPhone 3GS	Separated	Plastic
iPhone 4/4S	Fused	Glass
iPhone 5	Fused	Brushed aluminum
iPod touch 4	Fused	Silver aluminum
iPod touch 5	Fused	Brushed aluminum
iPad (2nd-4th gen)	Separated	Brushed aluminum
iPad mini	Separated	Brushed aluminum

Repair Options and DIY Strategies

If or when you are faced with repairing a broken iDevice screen, you have the following options available to you:

- Visit the Apple Store
- Hire a third party to replace the display
- Do it yourself (DIY)

Let's weigh the pros and cons of each approach, shall we?

Visit the Apple Store

If your iDevice has AppleCare+ then you are entitled to two free replacements, regardless of how the display damage occurred. In this case, I strongly suggest that you take advantage of the AppleCare+ coverage and not attempt a DIY repair—it simply makes no sense.

If your iDevice is out of warranty then Apple will repair...er...replace your iDevice (I'm smirking a bit as I type this, I must confess), but I'm afraid it's going to cost you. As of this writing in early 2013, the out-of-pocket charge breakdown with appropriate Apple.com page references for iPhones and iPads looks like this:

- iPhone 4S: $199 (http://is.gd/ZYJ0wb)
- iPhone 5: $229 (http://is.gd/ZYJ0wb)
- iPad 2: $249 (http://is.gd/7NUDNO)
- iPad 3rd/4th gen: $299 (http://is.gd/7NUDNO)
- iPad mini: $219 (http://is.gd/7NUDNO)

Ouch! Those high charges should justify the addition of AppleCare+ coverage to any new iDevice purchase, in my humble opinion.

Hire a Third Party to Replace the Display

If you are nervous about performing a front display or rear case replacement yourself, there are plenty of folks who will undertake the task for you—at a price.

My best words of advice are for you to *shop around* and *go with a technician who offers a warranty*. Skill levels and ethical foundations vary widely among iDevice technicians. If you can obtain a referral from a satisfied customer then all the better.

I suggest that you fire up Google or your favorite search engine and submit search strings that are akin to the following suggestions. See what you can discover. Perform some cost/benefit analysis to determine whether paying somebody to replace your iDevice screen or rear case is more cost-effective than paying Apple or performing the repair yourself.

- **iPhone 5 screen replacement service**
- **iPad 3 front glass replacement nashville** (substitute your own city for Nashville)
- **iPod touch 5 screen repair warranty**

Do It Yourself

Ah, now we come to the heart of the matter. You wouldn't be reading this book unless you had at least a passing interest in performing DIY repairs, am I correct?

We covered the step-by-steps for removing the display assemblies in the teardown chapters of this book. Here I present to you some targeted tips and tricks to assist you in your DIY screen repair journey.

Be Sure to Source the Correct Part(s)

Do you remember in Chapter 4, "iDevice Repair Best Practices," where I talk about how to identify iDevice models? It is crucial that you order a display assembly or rear case that was designed for your specific iDevice model. As I have discussed previously, whether a given replacement part is a "genuine" Apple Original Equipment Manufacturer (OEM) or a third-party knock-off isn't something that you have a heck of a lot of control over.

In my experience in performing iDevice parts replacements, I have just three criteria from which I work when sourcing parts:

- **Cost.** I obviously want to keep cost to a minimum in order to maximize my return on investment.
- **It works.** When I replace a display assembly, I need the iDevice to operate exactly the same way it did before the screen break.
- **The fit and finish are acceptable.** Nobody should be able to pick up a repaired iDevice and say, "This part is obviously not from the original unit."

What's weird, at least to me, in sourcing front display assemblies is how widely the costs vary. I've seen iPhone 5 display assemblies sold at iFixit for more than $100, and I've seen what appear to be the same kits sold on eBay for $30. What accounts for the price difference?

Well, iFixit stands behind their products with a warranty, and you might not get that with an Amazon- or eBay-sourced kit. iFixit also includes stuff that you don't ordinarily get with a replacement display assembly, such as precut adhesive strips. That counts for a lot, in my opinion.

As I told you before, when you find a good source for iDevice repair parts, do everything you can to cultivate that relationship—it's worth its weight in gold.

Some iPhones Are Easier to Repair Than Others

Replacing the front display assembly on the iPhone 3GS and iPhone 5 is a breeze because this is the first part that is removed from the device during the disassembly.

On the other hand, replacing the display or rear case on the iPhone 4 and iPhone 4S requires that you completely (and I do mean completely) disassemble the device in order to separate those parts from the rest of the phone. You can see this bitter truth in Figure 15.3.

FIGURE 15.3   To replace the iPhone 4/4S display, a full disassembly is required. (Photo courtesy of ifixit.com)

iPads Are Uniformly Awful in Terms of Display Replacement

I loathe performing display replacements on iPads with the fiery passion of a thousand burning suns. Why? Well, for one thing, the glass and digitizer combo is glued to the case extremely securely. For another thing, exerting the smallest amount of extra pressure when you try to lift the glass breaks said glass. Third, resolving a shattered front panel means not only removing the front glass, but also spending a lot of time with a spudger removing tiny glass particles from the gluey frame. This is not a fun way to spend your evenings at home, friends.

Be Sure to Purchase Adhesive Strips

You may be able to get away without adhesive strips with iPhone screen or rear case replacements, but you will almost certainly require some strips to securely re-fasten the iPad display assembly to the case. iFixit sells these strips precut per iDevice; very thoughtful! Figure 15.4 shows one of these products.

If Possible, Test the Display Before Reassembly

After you've connected the glass, digitizer, and LCD back to the iDevice logic board, power on the device to make sure that it works before you actually reseal the case. Of course, this isn't always possible, especially when you are dealing with the iPhone 4. However, I've saved myself quite a bit of time and unnecessary frustration performing these display "preflight" checks on iPad 2, 3, and 4 screen replacements that I've performed.

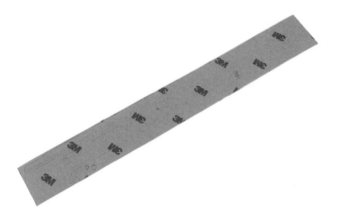

FIGURE 15.4   iFixit precut adhesive strips for the iPad.

Use a Microfiber Cloth and Blower to Remove Fingerprints and Dust

When I perform a front display replacement on an iPad, which as you know has a separate LCD panel, I get paranoid that I'll leave fingerprints, smudges, or dust particles on the LCD. Believe me, you don't want that.

Therefore, I suggest that you use a microfiber cloth and "puff" dust blower to ensure that the LCD remains crystal-clear. The "puff" blower is nothing more than a bulb syringe that you squeeze to jet air onto your target surface; Figure 15.5 shows a "puff" dust blower.

FIGURE 15.5   iFixit dust blower.

How to Minimize Damage to the Display/Rear Case

Ultimately, protecting the screen and rear case of your expensive iDevice boils down to being careful with it. Keep the device out of the hands of small children and pets. Keep the iDevice out of the rain. However, you and I both know there always exists the "X factor" that no amount of proactivity can ward against.

■ You can purchase plastic or film screen protectors; these help ward against scratches, but obviously won't prevent a full-on crack in the event of impact.

■ You can add a protective case to your iDevice to provide full coverage of the iDevice's case. The downside to these products is they can add unwanted bulk to these otherwise svelte devices. Moreover, some cases can actually obstruct the display partially (this is the case—pun intended—with my iPad mini leather case).

16

Replacing the Battery

The battery is a good candidate for a Do-It-Yourself (DIY) iDevice repair because Lithium-ion (Li-ion) batteries have a limited number of charge cycles and are therefore replaceable. Of course, Apple does not want customers to replace iDevice batteries themselves. Rather, Apple wants you to turn in your current iDevice for a new model, or pay for a battery replacement.

To that latter point, Apple has a published policy (http://is.gd/i773q6) concerning battery replacements. It works like this:

- The default hardware warranty covers the battery for the first year of ownership
- The AppleCare Protection Plan covers the battery for the second year of ownership
- For out-of-warranty situations, if an Apple Store Genius determines upon inspection that your iDevice's battery capacity has dropped below the 50 percent mark, he will perform a battery replacement for a fee. The fee schedule is
    - iPod nano: $59
    - iPod touch: $79
    - iPhone: $79
    - iPad: $99

As you know by now, however, the Apple Store never opens iDevice cases. Thus, you aren't going to get a battery replacement while you wait. The best you can hope for is either to send in your iDevice to the online Apple Store or hope that the genius at the Genius Bar swaps out your iDevice. In my experience, either outcome is equally likely to occur.

If you've read the book in full up to now then you already know the challenges that are inherent in DIY iDevice repair. You can more easily replace the battery on some iDevices than on others.

Before you take your screwdriver and opening tools in hand, however, you need answers to some preliminary questions:

- How do Li-ion batteries work, anyway?
- Is there any truth to the so-called battery "memory effect"?
- What do all the funky markings on iDevice batteries mean?

If nothing else, friends, you can use the information you glean in this chapter to impress your friends at the bar with your deep understanding of iDevice arcana.

What You Need to Know about Lithium-Ion Batteries

Batteries, in general, are devices that store a chemically reactive agent and discharge electrical energy at a fixed rate to power an associated electronic system.

Apple iDevices use Lithium-ion batteries (Li-ion). Li-ion batteries are called secondary batteries because they can be recharged; this is in contrast to primary batteries, which are disposable.

The Li-ion batteries that are present in Apple iDevices are configured in battery packs (also called pouches) that consist of several individual battery cells aligned in parallel. Figure 16.1 shows the battery from an iPhone 4S.

FIGURE 16.1 An iPhone 4S battery.

CAUTION

Boom, Baby!

Because pure Lithium is very reactive and prone to explosion (more on that later), you need to be careful when you work with iDevice batteries.

What Is the "Memory Effect"?

Many iDevice owners are afraid to recharge their iPods, iPhones, or iPads until their batteries are nearly depleted because they are afraid of the so-called battery "memory effect."

First, the good news: *Li-ion batteries are immune to the memory effect*. You are perfectly safe performing partial charges (that is, plugging in the iDevice when the battery has charge left in it).

Second, the "memory effect" was a side effect of older rechargeable batteries, such as nickel-cadmium, in which the battery retains less and less charge over time if it is not allowed to discharge completely.

Apple documents some good battery-related information on its website (http://www.apple.com/batteries/). Specifically, iDevice batteries operate on a "fast charge" principle in which the battery is charged to 80 percent capacity at an accelerated rate, after which the remaining 20 percent is "trickle-charged" at a slower rate. This is a good thing because you can get your depleted iDevices back up and running quickly.

The bad news is that Li-ion batteries have a fixed number of charge cycles before they fail. Apple defines "charge cycle" as a complete charge, from empty to 100 percent capacity.

Over time, you will notice that your iDevice battery capacity gradually decreases. This is normal operation of the battery; even rechargeable batteries are ultimately disposable.

NOTE

Environmental Hazard

Li-ion batteries present an environmental hazard. Because of this, never simply toss your depleted iDevice into the trash can. Apple itself sponsors an iDevice recycling program; check out the details at http://www.apple.com/recycling/.

Of course, the salient question for is, "How many charge cycles are iDevice batteries good for?" Table 16.1 shows Apple's published information on battery cycles.

TABLE 16.1 Apple's Stated Battery Cycles

iDevice Model	Rated Number of Full Charge Cycles before reaching 75-80 percent charge capacity
iPhone	400
iPod touch	400
iPad	1,000

Let's now turn our attention to understanding iDevice battery nomenclature. You probably wondered during the iDevice disassemblies, "What do all these crazy specifications printed on the battery pouch actually mean in practice?" It's now time to get you some answers!

Understanding iDevice Battery Specifications

Take a look at Figure 16.2, which shows the markings on the iPhone 5 battery pouch.

FIGURE 16.2 iPhone 5 battery markings.

From a performance standpoint, the most important specification listed is the *milliampere-hour*, abbreviated to mAh. The mAh rating of a Li-ion battery denotes its overall capacity. Thus, higher mAh values represent batteries with larger capacities and are therefore preferable to batteries of the same type with lower mAh values.

The mAH rating is comparable to the *watt hour* (Whr) value. Because there are so many variables at play when attempting to calculate an iDevice's battery capacity, I'll leave the mathematics for another book.

As you can see in Figure 16.2, an iOS device battery draws 3.72 volts internally from the standard Apple 5V power adapter.

I want to call your attention also to the iDevice battery's Apple Part Number (APN) value. APN is the value that you need to track carefully when you purchase a replacement battery for your depleted iDevice.

For the sake of completeness, Table 16.2 lists the Apple-provided battery capacity data for its current iDevice portfolio.

TABLE 16.2   Apple's Stated iDevice Battery Capacities

iDevice Model	Talk Time	Wi-Fi Web Browsing Time	Music Playing Time
iPhone 5	8 hours	10 hours	40 hours
iPod touch 5th generation	N/A	10 hours	40 hours
iPad 4th generation	N/A	10 hours	10 hours

Best Practices for iDevice Battery Use

Apple's published guidelines state that iDevice batteries operate best in a temperature zone from 32° to 95° Fahrenheit. The best practice, of course, is to keep your iDevice at room temperature (approximately 72° F) most of the time.

As mentioned earlier, it's okay to charge Li-ion batteries in partial cycles rather than doing the "full battery deplete then full recharge" dance that has unfortunately become semi-standard practice among iDevice owners.

To that point, however, Apple suggests "exercising" your battery by depleting it completely and performing a full recharge once per month.

Is it possible to overcharge an iDevice battery? Stated simply, no. Your iDevice simply stops charging when the battery reaches the 100 percent capacity mark.

In iOS 6, you can check our iDevice battery statistics in a variety of ways:

- Check out the battery usage indicator in the on-screen status bar
- Navigate to Settings, General, Usage, as shown in Figure 16.3
- Search for battery utilities in the App Store
- Search for battery utilities in the Cydia Store (jailbroken iDevices only)

Figure 16.3 shows an example of the Usage screen in iOS 6.

FIGURE 16.3   iOS 6 battery usage (and displaying battery percentage).

Exploding Batteries

Now, about the "my iPhone battery exploded!" issue. Is there any truth to this claim? Well, yes. The fact of the matter is that the Li-ion polymers that are contained in iDevice battery pouches can be unstable in certain conditions—for instance, if any of the following occurs:

- The iDevice is kept in extreme temperatures for extended periods of time.
- The owner puts undue pressure on the battery pouch either directly or through the device case.
- The electronics of the iDevice contain a manufacturing defect and cause a short or over-charging (and resultant excessive heat) to be produced.

The battery page could indeed swell and perhaps "pop," bursting the seams of your iDevice and possibly producing smoke and/or sparks.

The iPhone 3GS was known in particular for experiencing this type of battery failure. The salient question, of course, is, "What can I do to limit the possibility of a battery explosion from occurring?"

The answer to that question is, "Give your iDevice the environmental and physical respect it deserves and, barring the aforementioned possibility of an undetected manufacturer's defect, you should be at low risk for a battery explosion."

Maximizing Battery Life

To wrap up this section I've included a "laundry list" of methods for maximizing the battery life of your iDevice. Most of these tips involve suspending a certain functionality, which should come as no surprise to you.

- Suspend Wi-Fi
- Turn down screen brightness
- Shorten iDevice sleep time
- Disable push email
- Disable push notifications
- Use Airplane Mode

- Temporarily disable carrier service
- Turn off Bluetooth
- Suspend Location Services
- Disable data push
- Turn off music EQ

Some apps from the Apple or Cydia app stores can provide detailed feedback on battery life savings if you make some of the above tweaks. For instance, check out Battery Doctor in Figure 16.4.

FIGURE 16.4 Battery Doctor is available in the Apple App Store.

Performing Battery Replacements

Let's gauge the relative ease of iDevice DIY battery replacement by using the simple rating system that I developed, which is shown in Table 16.3. This table also points you to ifixit.com's instructions for performing battery replacements.

TABLE 16.3 Battery Replacement Difficulty Ratings

iDevice Model	Replacement Ease Rating	Soldering Required?	iFixit Replacement Procedure
iPhone 3GS	1	No	http://is.gd/sJ6ABg
iPhone 4S	0	No	http://is.gd/5zrwFu
iPhone 5	0	No	http://is.gd/Yf57Gp
iPod touch 4th generation	3	Yes	http://is.gd/8Kdpnf
iPad 3rd generation	2	No	http://is.gd/0Vr6NC

0 = Reasonably easy to replace the battery

1 = Neutral; neither too difficult nor too easy

2 = Difficult to replace the battery

3 = Almost impossible to replace the battery

NOTE

Check Back Later

As of this writing, iFixit battery replacement guides for the iPad 4th generation and the iPod touch 5th generation were not yet available. Please check ifixit.com periodically to confirm availability.

It should come as no surprise to you that the iPhones are by far the easiest iDevices to perform battery replacements on. The risk of damaging your iPhone is minimal when undertaking this parts replacement.

Unfortunately, replacing the battery in the iPad or any of the iPods is probably not worth your time and effort unless you are extremely desperate. The iPads, of course, require that you mess with the severely glued-on front panel assemblies. Also, the iPad batteries are themselves glued fast to the rear case.

The iPods are even more nightmarish. Recall that iPod batteries tend to be soldered to the logic board. This means you have to exercise your desoldering and soldering skills to make that repair.

The disassemblies that I provide in this book, when combined with the iFixit links in Table 16.3, should be more than enough information to assist you through most iDevice battery replacements.

That said, I want to present a series of best practice tips for performing successful battery swaps:

- **Watch those part numbers:** You can determine the Li-ion APN by inspecting the outside markings of the battery pouch. You can also obtain your battery APN through the Cydia App Store if you have a jailbroken iDevice; see http://is.gd/PNkSda for a list of available apps.

- **Carefully select your soldering equipment:** For those of you who are brave enough to attempt a battery replacement on an iPod, you need to purchase a soldering iron, desoldering braid, and solder. iFixit sells all of these components, and you are well-advised to purchase their stuff because it has been qualified for iDevice solder jobs. Here are some notes:

  - Use a 50-watt soldering iron; you don't want a gun that heats up too much or too little.
  - Use 1mm rosin core solder with a ~450° F melting point.
  - Use copper desoldering braid with flux.

- **Accept the likelihood of cosmetic damage, at least for iPods:** As mentioned earlier in this book where I discuss the disassemblies, Apple has gone to great lengths to prevent folks from opening up their iPods. You face an extraordinarily high probability of marring the case of your iPod when you open it (see Figure 16.5). You also gamble with the loss of factory "fit and finish"; this latter problem can be obviated somewhat with the judicious application of 3M adhesive tape to hold the darned thing together.

FIGURE 16.5   iPod nano case damage that occurred during a battery replacement. The two silver objects in the frame are metal case opening tools.

Replacing the Logic Board and/or Dock Connector

This chapter covers not only logic board replacements, but also Dock connector repair. Why? Well, to save white space in this book, for one reason. Kidding aside, I know that the Dock or Lightning connector in many iDevice models is permanently affixed to the logic board, which means that to replace a Dock connector, you must also replace the logic board.

As usual, I begin this chapter with the theoretical background. Then I provide you with the need-to-know tips and tricks for successfully swapping a logic board and/or Dock connector in your broken iDevice.

About the Logic Board

You can look at the logic board as the "brains" platform of an iDevice. Technically, the central processing unit (CPU) constitutes the "intelligence" of a computer. However the logic board is a component that consists of far more than just the CPU.

If you've performed a disassembly of an iPod, iPhone, or iPad then you have seen for yourself that the vast majority of hardware components (including the LCD, digitizer, battery, Wi-Fi antenna, and so forth) terminate to the logic board.

You can see an iPhone logic board in Figure 17.1.

Much is made in the news when Apple announces a new device as to which processor Apple includes in the logic board. Where exactly is the processor, you may ask? Apple frames the CPU in a slightly larger package called a system-on-a-chip, or SoC.

You can look at an SoC as a sort of mini-computer that generally consists of the main input/output logic of the entire system. For instance, iDevice SoCs include the following:

- CPU
- Memory (RAM)
- Persistent storage
- Analog-to-digital converter
- Encryption engine
- Graphics engine (graphics processing unit, or GPU)

FIGURE 17.1 An iPhone logic board. (Photo courtesy of ifixit.com.)

In Figure 17.2 you can see a manifest of the iPhone 5 logic board components, courtesy of our friends at iFixit.

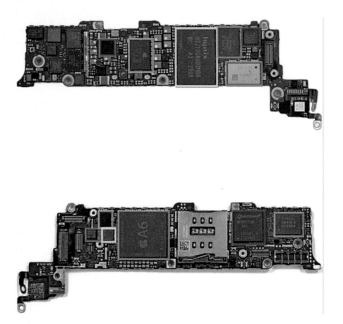

- Qualcomm PM8018 RF power management IC
- Hynix H2JTDG2MBR 128 Gb (16 GB) NAND flash
- Apple 338S1131 dialog power management IC*
- Apple 338S1117 Cirrus Logic Class D Amplifiers. The die inside is a Cirrus Logic device (second image) but it does not look like the audio codec.
- STMicroelectronics L3G4200D (AGD5/2235/G8SBI) low-power three-axis gyroscope—same as seen in the iPhone 4S, iPad 2, and other leading smart phones
- Murata 339S0171 Wi-Fi module
- STMicroelectronics LIS331DLH (2233/DSH/GFGHA) ultra low-power, high performance, three-axis linear accelerometer
- Texas Instruments 27C245I touch screen SoC
- Broadcom BCM5976 touchscreen controller
  - Rather than a single touchscreen controller, Apple went with a multi-chip solution to handle the larger screen size, à la iPad.
- Apple A6 application processor
- Qualcomm MDM9615M LTE modem
- Qualcomm RTR8600 Multi-band/mode RF transceiver, the same one found in the Samsung Galaxy S III

FIGURE 17.2 iPhone 5 SoC components. (Photo courtesy of ifixit.com.)

NOTE

It Bears Repeating

It's worth restating that the logic board is effectively the frame, or chassis, for the processor's SoC and associated components.

The good news about the logic board/system-on-a-chip situation is that all the core iDevice functionality is constrained to a single, user-replaceable part. The bad news is that, depending upon your iDevice, you might need to replace the entire logic board even if only a peripheral part (for instance, the Dock connector) goes bad.

iDevice Connectors

The Apple 30-pin Dock connector descends historically from the laptop docking station connectors that were used 15 to 20 years ago. In point of fact, the Dock connector first appeared in the 2003 iPod. Originally, the iPod cables were FireWire only. Eventually, Apple got the memo that Universal Serial Bus (USB) is the platform-independent standard. Thus, the Dock and even Lightning connectors to this very day employ the USB 2.0 standard. You can read more on the USB subject a bit later.

NOTE

Pay Attention to Product Names

Recall that you need to pay special attention to product names. Apple refers to the 30-pin Dock connector with a capital D. Please keep this in mind, even though you're likely to see references to "dock connectors" elsewhere on the Web.

I have not been the biggest fan of the 30-pin Dock connector for the following reasons:

- The connector is unidirectional, making proper connection difficult to perform in the dark
- The connector interface seats inside the iDevice in an unstable, somewhat shaky manner

On the other hand, the 30-pin connector can be used both to charge as well as sync data on supported iDevices. Moreover, the 30-pin connector carries just about any type of video or audio signal. In point of fact, I've given several successful presentations by connecting my iPad to a digital projector by means of the Apple 30-pin-to-DVI or 30-pin-to-VGA output adapters.

In 2012, Apple's long-standing commitment to the 30-pin Dock connector changed both fundamentally and quickly with its announcement of the Lightning interface. The following iDevices support the Lightning connector, and you can rest assured that all future iDevices will use this new connector type as well.

- iPhone 5
- iPad mini
- iPad 4th generation
- iPod touch 5th generation
- iPod nano 7th generation

Figure 17.3 shows the 30-pin and Lightning connectors side by side.

Lightning connector   30-pin Dock connector

FIGURE 17.3   Side-by-side comparison of the Lightning and 30-pin connectors.

In a nutshell, here is what I like about the Lightning connector:

- The Lightning connector is incredibly small and feels good in your hand.
- The Lightning connector is reversible! No more fumbling in the dark with plugging in your iDevice for overnight charging.
- The Lightning connector seats securely inside your iDevice. The connector head is one encapsulated piece instead of a row of wobbly pins.

In Table 17.1, I've summarized the major properties of the 30-pin Dock and Lightning connectors for easy reference.

TABLE 17.1 30-pin and Lightning Connector Comparison

Property	30-Pin Dock Connector	Lightning Connector
Number of pins	30	8
Reversible plug	No	Yes
Signaling	Audio + Video	Audio only
Data Transfer Rate	480 Mbps (USB 2.0)	480 Mbps (USB 2.0)
Power Delivery	12 watts	12 watts

Two important, additional points to consider with regard to the Lightning connector are

- Lightning operates at USB 2.0, not USB 3.0 speeds
- Lightning has no "video out" capability

Given that USB 2.0 has a 480 megabits per second (Mbps) transfer rate and USB 3.0 has a 5 gigabits per second (Gbps) transfer rate, it seems strange to me that Apple hasn't made the Lightning interface work with USB 3.0, or even Apple's and Intel's own Thunderbolt interface. Even more puzzling is the fact that USB 3.0 is backward compatible with USB 2.0.

To Apple's credit, they probably bypassed using micro USB as the interface because micro USB can deliver only 9 watts of power, and iPads need at least 10 watts.

A bit of silver lining here is that you can still use Dock-era chargers with Lightning USB cables in order to charge your iDevices.

As a teacher, I have presented material to my students several times by using my iPad 2 with a trusty Dock-to-DVI or Dock-to-VGA video adapter (shown in 17.4).

FIGURE 17.4 The 30-pin interface supports video out to a variety of monitor interfaces.

If you can believe it, the Lightning interface (at least as of this writing in early 2013) does not support "video out" signaling. This means you cannot use a Lightning-equipped iDevice to display video on a computer monitor, digital projector, or television screen without (you guessed it) the purchase of yet another adapter.

Apple sells a Lightning-to-HDMI adapter that, at least on paper, enables you to mirror your iDevice display to an HDMI-capable television or monitor. However, the Apple Store reviews on this technology are mixed.

Sadly, those of you who invested heavily in iDevice accessories that include the standard Dock connector will likely spend a pretty penny purchasing signal converters.

For your reference, here is a list of Lightning adapters that were available at the time of this writing. Here is a list of the adapters that are shown in Figure 17.5:

- Lightning to 30-pin Adapter (with and without cable)
- Lightning to USB Cable
- Lightning to Micro USB Adapter
- Lightning to Digital AV Adapter
- Lightning to VGA Adapter
- Lightning to USB Camera Adapter
- Lightning to SD Card Camera Reader

FIGURE 17.5 Apple is more than willing to sell you adapters to get the Lightning interface "talking to" your current Dock-enabled hardware.

TIP

Apple's Grip Tightens

According to the well-respected technology website Ars Technica (http://
is.gd/3WPCaq), Apple included an on-board authentication chip inside the Lightning
connector plug that makes is very difficult for iDevice peripheral manufacturers to
make their accessories without Apple's approval.

Repair Advice

You might have the following question: "Given that so much of the iDevice functionality
hinges on the logic board, how can I test to verify that a logic board is, indeed, bad?"

The answer to that question is straightforward: Pull the suspected bad logic board from the
source device and install it in a known-good device.

Remember that if you want to become a productive iDevice tech, you need to make a
substantial investment for tools and parts. Some of these "parts" can be considered known-
good iDevices that you can use for diagnostics such as these.

If you put a suspected bad logic board into a known-good iDevice and that device fails to
boot then you can state conclusively that you need to replace the logic board on the ailing
device. The same "swap" rule applies to the Dock Connector for iDevices that allow the
Dock connector to be separated from the logic board.

Speaking of Dock connectors, let me provide you with a "cheat sheet" that you can use to
instantly determine whether the connector can be replaced on an iDevice independently of
the logic board.

TABLE 17.2   Relationship of Dock Connector to the Logic Board on Select
iDevices

iDevice Model	Is the Dock Connector Separable from the Logic Board?	Notes
iPod nano 7th generation	No	
iPod touch 5th generation	No	
iPhone 5	Yes	Lightning connector, headphone jack, and cel-lular antenna exist on a single assembly
iPad 4th generation	Yes	Lightning connector has its own ribbon cable
iPad mini	No	

In my experience, replacing an iDevice logic board is a pretty straightforward operation. The only tough spots are the soldering requirement for certain iDevices, and the difficulty in removing the display assembly on iPads.

Overall, the best advice I can give you for sourcing replacement logic boards is to obtain a vendor referral from a trusted source. For instance, in a recent eBay auction search for an iPhone 4S logic board I obtained results that were priced from $13.50 to more than $200. That price variance is suspect, to say the least.

If you want or need to perform advanced diagnostics on iDevice Dock connectors and logic boards, then you need to use a multimeter. A multimeter is a hardware testing device that measures several electrical properties, including

- Resistance
- Voltage
- Current

Theoretically, you should be able to use any ol' multimeter to test iDevice electrical components. However, the good folks at Red Fish Instruments (http://redfishinstruments. com) have developed an iDevice-specific multimeter called the iDVM Multimeter. Figure 17.6 shows you this product.

FIGURE 17.6   The Red Fish Instruments iDVM Multimeter.

The iDVM is a combination of hardware and software. The iDVM hardware instrument communicates with your iDevice wirelessly, and reports its data findings to an associated iOS app. Pretty cool, huh?

Tips and Tricks for Logic Board Replacements

Let's conclude this chapter with some targeted advice concerning things you should watch out for when you attempt a logic board replacement on recent iPhones, iPads, and iPods.

iPhone 5

iPhone 5 (and iPhone 4/4S, for that matter) logic boards are the easiest logic boards to replace in any iOS device. Sure, you have to field-strip the iDevice practically to the bare metal. You also have to remove a large number of microscopic screws. However, you have no glue or solder joints impeding your progress—in iDevice repair, that is a good thing.

The best advice I can give you for iPhone 5 logic board repairs are as follows:

- **Take all the time you need in re-seating the logic board**. We know by now that Apple engineers make use of every square centimeter inside an iPhone chassis. Leaving the logic board the tiniest bit askew—which is to say, not 100 percent flush—will wreak havoc later on in the reassembly, particularly with the display alignment.

- **Be respectful of the interconnect cables and camera connections**. Don't just yank up the logic board from the frame during disassembly in an (understandable) moment of frustration. The interconnect cables are there for a reason, and these connectors, as well as those for the rear-facing camera, need to be seated properly during reassembly to ensure the iDevice will work properly post-reassembly.

I show you the relationship between the iPhone 5 logic board and the interconnect cables in Figure 17.7.

FIGURE 17.7   Treat the rear-facing camera and interconnect cables and connectors with care during a logic board replacement. (Courtesy of ifixit.com.)

iPad 3rd and 4th Generation

Logic board replacements on the 3rd and 4th generation iPads are extraordinarily difficult. As we've discussed previously, removing the glass panel/digitizer assembly runs a high risk of shattering the glass.

The best advice I can offer you, besides carefully noting which screws and connectors go with which components, is to stock up on Kapton tape. As you can see in Figure 17.8, Apple uses a copious amount of Kapton tape and adhesive to secure cables and connectors to the logic board and rear case.

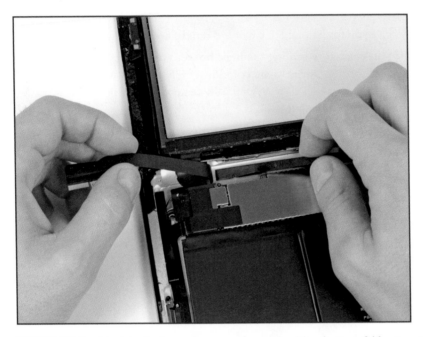

FIGURE 17.8 iPad logic boards are secured with plenty of Kapton tape and adhesive glue. (Photo courtesy of ifixit.com.)

iPad mini

All of the standard precautions that apply to the full-sized iPads apply in turn to the iPad mini. With the mini, however, I advise you to remember that the Lightning connector is soldered to the logic board. This is shown in Figure 17.9.

iPod touch 5th Generation

In the iPod touch 5th generation, the logic board, battery, front-facing camera, Lightning connector, speaker, headphone jack, and Home button are all soldered together into an individual assembly. Fun, fun!

FIGURE 17.9   In the iPad mini, the Lightning connector is soldered to the logic board.

Therefore, the biggest disappointment in replacing the logic board on the iPod touch is that you can either:

- Buy a replacement logic board assembly, with all connected hardware.
- Use your soldering equipment to desolder and resolder the existing hardware components to the new logic board.

Figure 17.10 shows the removal of the iPod touch 5th generation logic board assembly.

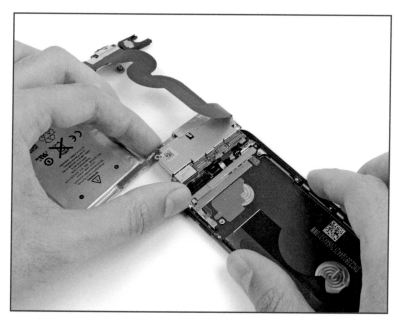

FIGURE 17.10   Several components are soldered to the iPod touch logic board. (Photo courtesy of ifixit.com.)

Recovering Data from Your Broken iDevice

A wise teacher once told me, "Tim, with iDevices there are many shades of 'dead.'" What this person meant is that a customer's complaint of "My iPhone is dead" conveys practically no useful information to the technician.

Some common questions in response to the "My iDevice is dead" statement include the following:

- Does your iDevice not turn on at all, or does it turn on but doesn't do anything?
- When did you last charge the iDevice?
- Did any liquid get on or inside the iDevice?
- How long has the device not worked?
- What changed in the iDevice's environment between when it last worked and when it didn't?

The list of open-ended diagnostic questions goes on and on. In my experience, most customers express concern that they won't be able to get to their data anymore now that the iDevice is apparently bricked.

This chapter starts with a detailed consideration of how iDevice users can minimize their risk of data loss in the event of iDevice failure.

Next it describes some scenarios that embrace various forms of iDevice "deadness" and provides you with some strategies for gaining access to iDevice data. For instance, I show you how to move the disk drive from one iDevice to another and mount the disk in the second device for the purposes of data retrieval.

Finally, this chapter shows you how easy it is to extract data from iTunes backups. This conversation involves information security and data encryption and dovetails nicely with what's covered in Chapter 19, "Before You Sell, Donate, or Recycle Your iDevice."

Protecting Your Data by Using Apple Services

In a best-case scenario, you (or your customer) avail yourselves of Apple's services to ensure that your data remains available to you on all of your iDevices. After all, redundancy (that is, keeping data stored in several locations at once) is a cornerstone of fault tolerance in the IT industry.

Our two best friends in this regard are iCloud and iTunes Match.

iCloud

As you probably know, iCloud is Apple's cloud-based storage service. The service began life as .Mac before becoming MobileMe. "Cloud-based storage" means that the following iDevice user data is stored on Apple's servers:

- Purchased music, movies, TV shows, apps, and books
- Photos and videos in the Camera Roll
- Device settings (for example, Phone Favorites, Wallpaper, and Mail, Contacts, Calendar accounts)
- Home screen and app organization
- App data (not the apps themselves; only data stored within the apps)
- Messages (iMessage, SMS, and MMS)
- Ringtones
- Visual Voicemails

In other words, all the contents of an iTunes-based iDevice backup are included in iCloud backups.

What's ingenious about this service is that you can retrieve the cloud-based resources on any Mac computer or iDevice that shares the same Apple ID. Isn't that great?

free iCloud You already know how convenient iCloud backups are. Please do everything you can to encourage your clients to use their free iCloud accounts and purchase additional storage if necessary to back up all of their data.

iTunes Match

cloud iTunes Match is a subscription service in which you store your iTunes music library in the cloud on Apple's servers. You can then pull down that content to all of your Macs and iDevices. If you listen to music or audiobooks much, like I do, then this service more than pays for itself.

You also have the security of knowing that a dead iDevice isn't going to interrupt your music and media enjoyment one little bit. You can repair or replace the device, enable iTunes Match in iOS, and BOOM! You have your library back.

Retrieving User Data from a "Dead" iDevice

Remember the watchwords with which I opened up this chapter: "Dead" is a relative term with iDevices. If you have a waterlogged iDevice and if you've been studying this book, you now know how to address that situation. (Refer to Chapter 14, "Addressing Water Damage," for a refresher.)

If you have an iDevice that won't power on then you now know how to disassemble the unit. Remember that the permanent, solid-state storage is contained in a chip on the logic board. You can therefore take the logic board out of the failed iDevice and install it into the chassis of a known-good device.

Of course, the aforementioned procedure won't work if you have a damaged logic board; in that case, I hope that you have a recent backup to fall back on.

When you are able to power on the iDevice, you need to connect it to iTunes, take a backup, and then use a third-party utility to drill into the iTunes backup archive and review its contents. I cover that procedure later in this chapter.

Retrieving User Data from a Live iDevice

You may find yourself in a situation where you need to retrieve media from a physically intact iDevice, but for whatever reason you can't get to the PC or Mac with which you sync the device. As we see in a moment, Apple enables you to sync your iDevice with one, and only one, instance of iTunes. What are we to do?

Music

I once supported iOS devices at a local high school in Nashville. Without question, the biggest concern the kids had when they brought their broken iPods to me was, "Mr. Warner, can you please get my music back?"

This was before iCloud or iTunes Match, so there was the very real possibility that the 40 hours the student spent ripping his or her CDs into the iTunes library might actually go up the flue.

Did you ever wonder why iTunes let you sync your iDevice's music library with only one computer at a time? How many of you have seen the iTunes message shown in Figure 18.1 when you tried to pull music from an iPod by syncing it with another computer?

Are you sure you want to remove existing music, movies, TV shows, books, and tones from this iPod and sync with this iTunes library?

Music, movies, TV shows, books, and tones synced to "Tim's iPod touch 5" from other iTunes libraries will be removed and items will be synced from this iTunes library.

Cancel   Remove and Sync

FIGURE 18.1   iTunes lets you sync an iDevice with only one computer.

The answer to this question consists of four letters: RIAA. When Apple introduced the iPod in 2001, they were (and are) subject to media usage restrictions from the Recording Industry Association of American (RIAA) and other music industry-affiliated groups.

From the RIAA's perspective, the one device/one computer synchronization limit made sense. After all, what would stop somebody from sharing their iTunes library with their friends by dumping the music on multiple host computers?

The typical iDevice customer/music enthusiast can't imagine the licensing details that go on behind the scenes to support technologies like iTunes Wi-Fi home sharing (find out more at http://is.gd/HUpubd) or iTunes Match. I have some very good friends who work for Broadcast Music International (BMI) here in Nashville, so I have some privileged insight into the situation.

The good news is that third-party development has stepped in to fill the void (although Apple has filled itself with iTunes Match, frankly) by providing us with software to retrieve our media libraries from our iDevices.

Here is a list of some of the most popular iDevice music library retrieval products:

- AnyTrans (shown in Figure 18.2; Windows only; http://is.gd/7HnJzT)
- iRip (Mac and Windows; http://is.gd/y34VVM)
- Senuti (Mac only; http://is.gd/pYFE6S)

FIGURE 18.2   AnyTrans gives you full control over your iDevice music library.

In closing, I want to let you know that you can always mount the iDevice as a disk in Windows or Mac and access the music library folders directly. This procedure might work as a last-ditch effort when you are pressed for time.

However, pulling music "in the raw" like this means that you lose all of the meaningful metadata surrounding your music library, especially objects like playlists, ratings, and listen counts. That's the chief advantage (besides ease of use, naturally) that third-party solutions offer us.

Photos

As long as your iDevice doesn't have passcode protection enabled, or you know the passcode, you can mount the iDevice as a camera in Windows and Mac and import your Camera Roll pictures, as shown in Figure 18.3. That's all well and good if all you need are the photos you snapped by using your iDevice. However, what if you need ALL of the photos that you previously synced to a computer?

NOTE

What's That Again?

This bears repeating: the "Camera Roll" refers to pictures taken with the device itself. The Camera Roll does not include photo albums that you manage from iPhoto or a Windows photo management tool and synchronize with your iDevice.

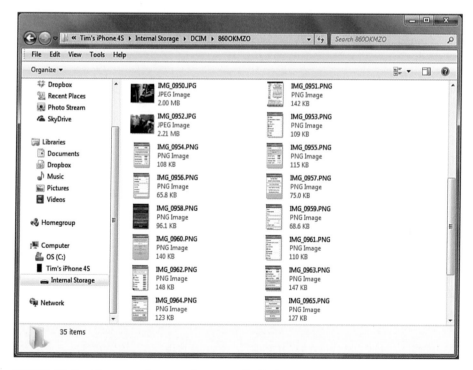

FIGURE 18.3   You can import Camera Roll pictures to your computer without iTunes.

Again, third-party utilities are your best friend for pulling part or all your iDevice photo data. Here are three popular examples of this type of software:

■ CopyTrans Photo (Windows only; http://is.gd/OwpzKf)

■ SyncPod (Mac only; http://is.gd/1uB6II)

■ iExplorer (Mac and Windows; http://is.gd/Rzm0mS)

The Rest of Your Stuff

Could I be a little more vague? "The rest of your stuff?" Really? Allow me to be more specific. What if you need to retrieve the following elements from your iDevice:

■ Contacts

■ Calendar items

■ SMS and iMessage messages

■ Voice recordings

■ Videos

■ Voicemail recordings

■ Notes

■ Call history

■ Location data

The best way to do this is to take a backup of the iDevice and (yes, again) use a good third-party utility to extract meaningful content from the iTunes backup. Remember that iTunes backups are ridiculously obfuscated; they are nearly impossible to interpret without the assistance of a separate tool.

Here's the procedure:

1. Connect the target iDevice to a host computer via the USB cable.

2. If the iDevice is passcode-locked, you see the message shown in the Figure 18.4. If you don't have the passcode then you can stop right here—you're hosed. I discuss passcodes more in just a little while.

3. Take a manual backup of the device. Refer to Chapter 3, "Protecting Your iDevice User Data and Settings," for a reminder of how to do that.

4. Start a third-party iDevice backup extractor program. Here are some suggestions:

    ■ iPhone Backup Extractor (Mac and Windows; http://is.gd/XXKljk)

    ■ Wondershare Data Recovery for iTunes (Mac only; http://is.gd/Pwub5f)

    ■ Wondershare Dr. Fone (Windows only; http://is.gd/wOtVsN)

FIGURE 18.4   You need to know the iDevice passcode to connect the device to iTunes.

I have had excellent luck with iPhone Backup Extractor. The program works equally well in Windows and in OS X, and you can drill into iTunes backups from iPhones, iPads, and iPod touches. You can see the user interface and some results of backup extraction in Figures 18.5 and 18.6.

FIGURE 18.5   The iPhone Backup Extractor tool makes short work of digging into iDevice backups.

FIGURE 18.6   The iTunes backup contents in human-readable form.

Passcode Security

I'll tell you, friends—the best way for you to protect your iDevice against theft and data loss is to use a passcode (see Figure 18.7). Let me repeat:

> *Please set a passcode lock on your iDevice so that unauthorized parties cannot view your personal data.*

Not only does a passcode lock protect your iDevice against unauthorized local access, but as described earlier in the chapter, you cannot connect an iDevice to iTunes and perform a data dump without knowing the passcode.

Yes, there exist third-party solutions that can (and do) make short work of decrypting the passcode lock. One notable example is XRY from Micro Systemation (http://is.gd/XCim6v). This is extremely powerful mobile device forensic software that is thankfully available for purchase only by law enforcement, the military, or intelligence agencies.

When you think of it cryptographically, a four-digit passcode gives an attacker a 1 in 10,000 (0000 to 9999) chance of guessing the code. Please consider adding an additional layer of security to your iDevice by using a complex passcode. Here's the procedure:

1. On your iDevice, navigate to Settings, General, Passcode Lock.

2. Switch the Simple Passcode option to Off.

3. Set a more complex passcode. You can use alphanumeric characters and make the passcode as long as you want.

FIGURE 18.7   The passcode prompt on an iDevice.

From now on, you can use the traditional soft keyboard when you are challenged to enter your passcode. This interface is shown in Figure 18.8.

FIGURE 18.8   You can further protect your iDevice by using a complex passcode.

It makes sense to ask your customer to disable the passcode lock prior to handing the iDevice to you for service. But what if the screen is cracked and you cannot enter a passcode at all?

In this case, you can boot the iDevice into Device Firmware Update (DFU) mode and restore the iOS firmware from an iPhone Software File (IPSW) archive.

DFU mode and IPSWs are common terms for iOS jailbreakers. However, you can also employ this special recovery mode to manually restore an iDevice to the current or potentially earlier firmware version.

Here's the procedure:

1. Download the IPSW file for your target iOS version. Here are some reliable sources for obtaining the files:

   ■ iClarified.com (http://is.gd/h9iyWN)

   ■ OSXDaily.com (http://is.gd/smSKSM)

   ■ IPSWDownloader (http://is.gd/Tl9Uzq)

NOTE

Worth the Cost

If you join the Apple iOS Developer Program ($99 per year; http://is.gd/7uLP2G) you're allowed to download any IPSW file directly from Apple's servers.

2. Plug your iDevice into your host computer and start up iTunes. Make sure your iDevice is powered off.

3. Hold down the Sleep/Power button and the Home button for 10 seconds and then release the Sleep/Power button while continuing to hold the Home button. After a few seconds the iDevice screen goes black and you see the iTunes interface messages shown in Figure 18.9.

By booting the iDevice into DFU mode, you bypass the installed iOS. In effect, this is like booting a PC by using a startup DVD instead of the local hard drive.

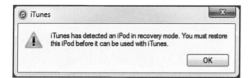

FIGURE 18.9   iTunes notification that you are in DFU mode.

NOTE

DFU = Recovery Mode

iTunes software refers to DFU mode as "recovery mode." Be aware that these two terms are synonymous.

4. In iTunes, hold down the Option (OS X) or Ctrl (Windows) keys and then click Restore. Instead of instructing iTunes to download and apply the latest firmware for your iDevice, you are instead given the opportunity to browse for an IPSW file.

5. Locate and select your target IPSW file. iTunes takes over, restoring the given firmware version.

NOTE

Save Those SHSH Blobs

You can only restore iOS firmware images for which you have SHSH blobs available on your iDevice. To be proactive, you might want to use Tiny Umbrella (http:// thefirmwareumbrella.blogspot.com/) to save your target iDevice's blobs regularly so that you can potentially downgrade your iOS version if necessary.

6. If you run into a problem, you can take the iDevice out of DFU mode and perform a normal boot by holding the Sleep/Power and Home buttons at the same time until you see the Apple logo. Let go of both buttons simultaneously.

7. After you have the firmware reinstalled, the passcode should be cleared. You can then restore user content by using an iTunes or an iCloud backup.

Encrypted Backups, Anyone?

iTunes allows an iDevice user to encrypt his or her local backups. All you have to do is check the **Encrypt local backup** option in on your iDevice **Summary** page in iTunes 11.

After you enable encrypted backups, you are prompted to protect each backup with a password. You need this password in order to restore an iTunes backup in the future.

CAUTION

Don't Forget Your Password!

If you lose or forget your password, it is impossible to use the encrypted iTunes backups.

iPhone Backup Extractor can pull data from encrypted iTunes backups, but again, you need to know the password. By way of review, recall that iTunes stores backup archives in the following locations by default:

- **OS X:** ~/Library/Application Support/MobileSync/Backup/
- **Windows 7/Windows 8:** \Users*username*\AppData\Roaming\Apple Computer\ MobileSync\Backup\

In case you were wondering, iCloud backups are encrypted both in transit and on Apple's servers, with email and notes data as exceptions. For more information, see the following online resources:

- **Apple Support article:** "iCloud security and privacy overview" (http://is.gd/8KKV03)
- **Blog post:** "Ask Ars: how safe is my data stored in iCloud?" (http://is.gd/4mjkGi)

Before You Sell, Donate, or Recycle Your iDevice

In performing research for this book, I stopped at Nashville's most popular used media store in search of second-hand iDevices. Boy, were my expectations exceeded! Within 20 minutes I left the store with both arms full of iPhones, iPod touches, and iPods.

I arrived home and immediately set about charging up the sundry Apple mobile hardware. You can't imagine my surprise, however, when I powered on the iDevices and discovered that not a single one was erased.

At my fingertips I had so much personal information it made me feel guilty and uncomfortable using the devices. We are talking about

- Previous owner's name and contact information
- Fully populated contact cards
- Overflowing Photo Stream and Camera Roll pictures
- SMS and iMessage text messages
- Email messages

The list goes on. Needless to say, I was aghast, and I quickly performed a secure erase on all my "new" iDevices. (By the end of this chapter, you'll know how to perform a secure erase as well.)

To be honest, I wasn't sure who was more at fault for not erasing the devices prior to offering them for sale: the original owners or the secondhand shop staff.

In my opinion, understanding the hows and whys of iDevice reset and erasure is a core skill that every iDevice owner needs to have. The following are some of the common reasons why you might transfer ownership of your iDevice:

- You plan to gift or donate your iDevice.
- You plan to sell the device.
- You plan to take the device in for repairs and don't want techs viewing your data.
- You plan to turn in your device for an upgrade.

Before you even seriously ponder erasing and resetting your iDevice, it should go without saying that you need to ensure that you have at least one known-good iTunes or iCloud backup at the ready should you change your mind after the erasure completes.

First I want to dispel some common myths regarding data deletion.

Is Deleted Stuff Actually Deleted?

Traditionally, data that has been deleted from a mechanical or solid-state hard drive is not actually deleted. Instead, the host operating system (iOS for our purposes) simply *marks* that data as having been deleted. Consequently, unless the operating system overwrites those blocks with fresh (or even pseudo-random) data, it is very possible to retrieve the blocks' original contents.

NOTE

A Word About File Systems

In case you are interested, the file system that is used by iOS devices is Hierarchical File System, Extended (HFSX). HFSX is an extension of HFS+ that supports file and folder name case sensitivity.

Encryption, Your iDevice, and You

The good news is that as long as your iDevice runs at least iOS 5, all persistent data stored in flash memory is encrypted by default. Stated simply, *encryption* refers to the conversion of human-readable data to (for lack of a better word) jibberish.

iOS devices use the industry-standard Advanced Encryption Standard (AES) algorithm. You can consider an algorithm to be a complex mathematical formula. You take human-readable data, combine it with a unique, private key (essentially a really long number), and run it through the AES formulae. The end result is ciphertext.

The AES cryptographic engine is called *hardware encryption* by Apple because it consists of a system on a chip (SoC) located on the iDevice's logic board (specifically in the address path between flash storage and RAM).

iPhones, iPads, and iPod touches contain two 256-bit AES keys that are stored locally on each device and are inaccessible to system users. One key, called the Group ID (GID) key, is shared by all iPhones, iPads, and iPod touches. The other key, called the User ID (UID) key, is unique for each iDevice.

These encryption keys are not used directly by iOS to encrypt and decrypt data. Instead, iOS uses the GID and UID to generate in-memory keys that actually perform the cryptographic work on the device.

NOTE

Practice Makes Perfect

If you want to practice your iOS jailbreaking and mobile device forensics skills, you can check out the SecurityLearn blog post "Extracting AES keys from iPhone" at http://is.gd/IzMDFD.

Now you can see, I'm sure, how important (and potentially vulnerable) those encryption/decryption keys are on your iDevice. Apple provides a related security technology called *data protection* in which you can protect your hardware encryption keys with a single passcode.

Follow these steps to enable data protection by configuring a passcode for your device:

1. Tap Settings, General, Passcode Lock.

2. Use the following steps to define a passcode.

   a. Turn the passcode on

   b. Create and confirm your passcode

   c. Set passcode complexity options

3. Verify the configuration by scrolling down to the bottom of the screen and observing that the text **Data Protection Is Enabled** is visible (called out in Figure 19.1).

What's cool about Apple's hardware encryption is that you can simply nuke the encryption keys to render the entire disk unreadable. The key deletion occurs almost instantly, as well.

However, you'll observe that when you perform a full erase of an iOS device, the process can take upwards of several hours. What's going on here?

As it happens, iOS follows up the encryption key deletion with a full pass of device storage, overwriting the contents of each and every block. This process can take several minutes to several hours, depending upon the storage capacity of your iDevice.

The nutshell summary of all this information is that you can derive comfort in the fact that when you remove all data and settings from your iDevice, you are in fact securely erasing the device such that even a world-class forensics team would be very unlikely to recover data from that device.

In the following section, I show you how easy it is to securely erase your iDevice.

FIGURE 19.1   Use the passcode to protect your hardware encryption keys.

Preparing Your iDevice for Transfer— Local Method

Before you erase the contents of your iDevice, please ensure that

- You made a complete backup by using either iTunes or iCloud.
- iMessage is turned off. You want to avoid the possibility of the device's next owner receiving your iMessage content, so you need to unlink the device from your Apple ID. You can do this by navigating to Settings, Messages, iMessage and sliding iMessage to Off.
- You removed your SIM card from the iDevice. Leave the tray behind, however, so that the device's next owner can insert his or her own SIM card to gain carrier network access.

Use the following steps to perform the erasure from your iDevice:

1. Navigate to Settings, General, Erase, and tap Erase All Content and Settings. As you can see in Figure 19.2, you are prompted to confirm your choice.

FIGURE 19.2   Initiating an erase on an iPhone.

2. When the device returns from the secure erasure and reboots, you're prompted to set up the iDevice as a new device. At this point you are ready to transfer the iDevice to its new owner (see Figure 19.3).

FIGURE 19.3   A factory-fresh iPhone, ready for its new owner.

Preparing Your iDevice for Transfer–Remote Method

As you obviously know, your iDevice contains sensitive data that you do not want to fall into the wrong (that is to say, anybody else's) hands. What recourse do you have if, heaven forbid, a malicious individual were to steal your beloved iDevice?

Alternatively, what if you sell your iDevice and realize afterward that you forgot to erase all content and settings?

The good news is that as long as the following items are true, you can perform a remote wipe on your iDevice:

- The iDevice is powered on.
- The iDevice is reachable via carrier network or Wi-Fi.
- The iDevice hasn't had the Find My iPhone/Find My iPad/Find My iPod iCloud service disabled.

NOTE

Find My iPhone No Longer Works

After you remotely wipe an iDevice, you lose the ability to determine the device's location by using Find My iPhone.

To perform a remote wipe via a web browser and the iCloud website, use the following steps:

1. Open a Web browser, navigate to icloud.com and log into the service with your Apple ID and password.

2. From within iCloud, click Find My iPhone (wonky name, I realize, because you can locate iPads and iPod touches here as well).

3. Open the Devices menu and select the target iDevice.

4. In the device's Info window, click Erase iPhone, Erase iPad, or Erase iPod, depending upon the device (see Figure 19.4).

5. Enter your Apple ID to confirm your decision. The iDevice is then securely erased immediately.

FIGURE 19.4   Remotely wiping an iDevice by using iCloud.

Corporate Solutions

Apple has historically not been known for its enterprise friendliness. For instance, I still have nightmares in which I flash back to my past experiences in integrating Apple's Open Directory with Microsoft's Active Directory.

Nevertheless, many information technology (IT) departments realize the value, not to mention the overarching popularity, of iOS devices, and as such IT decision makers increasingly find themselves faced with distributing, managing, and supporting iPhones in their enterprise networks. Many of these networks are Windows-only, which poses additional challenges.

A detailed discussion of enterprise-level remote iDevice wiping is far beyond the scope of this volume. However, I thought it instructive to at least let you know what primary options are out there in the arena of remote device wipes.

Microsoft shops that need to support iPhones can use Microsoft Exchange Server (http://is.gd/75FEnc) and Microsoft ActiveSync to enroll, manage, and perform remote wipes on iPhones. For those who don't know, Exchange Server is Microsoft's enterprise messaging platform; it offers corporate email, shared calendaring, task lists, and deep integration with other collaboration platforms such as Voice over IP (VoIP) telephony and SharePoint web portals.

ActiveSync is a long-standing Microsoft proprietary protocol that enables mobile phones to synchronize content with Exchange Server.

If a business is fortunate enough to have deployed at least one Apple OS X Server (http://is.gd/5mLDZt) box in its environment then IT administrators can leverage the Profile Manager tool to perform remote wipes on enrolled iOS devices. Profile Manager is a web-based management application that supports full control of any Apple hardware in use within the organization. A screenshot from the Profile Manager interface is shown in Figure 19.5.

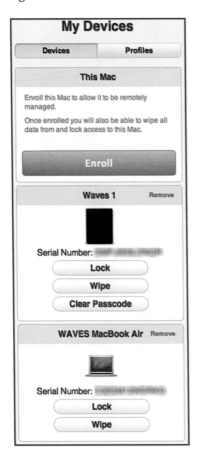

FIGURE 19.5   You can use Profile Manager to perform a remote wipe of a managed iDevice.

Disposal and Associated Environmental Concerns

iDevices, like many types of portable electronic equipment, contains glass and heavy metals that are destructive to the environment. Actually, if some of these metals—such as cadmium, lead, nickel, mercury, manganese, lithium, zinc, arsenic, antimony, beryllium, and copper—leach into ground water, they can produce sickness and death in plants, animals, and humans.

The Lithium-Ion (Li-ion) batteries in your iDevices present another environmental hazard. Although these units do not contain heavy metals, they do indeed pose an environmental fire hazard.

In all seriousness, you need to take iDevice disposal seriously and not simply toss your broken or unwanted hardware into the trash.

You should know that Apple itself instituted an incentive program to encourage you to turn in your unwanted mobile hardware to either your nearest Apple Store or online at http://is.gd/rclJAK.

Be aware of the following facts concerning the Apple iPod and Mobile Phone Recycling Program:

- Apple provides environmentally friendly disposal of any manufacturer's mobile phones.
- If you recycle your iPod then Apple gives you a 10 percent discount toward the purchase of another iPod.
- If you recycle your iPhone then you could be given an Apple Gift Card worth the old phone's fair market value. (You can read more information at http://is.gd/j4jKG8.)

INDEX

CHECK OUT MUST-HAVE BOOKS IN THE BESTSELLING MY... SERIES

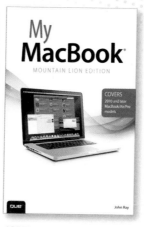

Full-Color, Step-by-Step Guides

The "My..." series is a visually rich, task-based series to help you get up and running with your new device and technology, and tap into some of the hidden, or less obvious, features. The organized, task-based format allows you to quickly and easily find exactly the task you want to accomplish, and then shows you how to achieve it with minimal text and plenty of visual cues.

**Visit quepublishing.com/mybooks to learn more
about the My... book series from Que.**

quepublishing.com

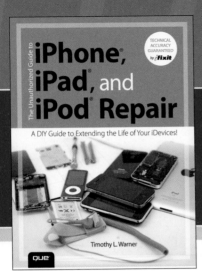

FREE
Online Edition